Contents

Preface 4

Introduction 5

Chapter 1: 1901-1910 24

Chapter 2: 1911-1920 33

Chapter 3: 1921-1930 57

Chapter 4: 1931-1940 114

Chapter 5: 1941-1950 162

Chapter 6: 1951-1960 207

Chapter 7: 1961-1970 249

Chapter 8: 1971-1980 277

Chapter 9: 1981-1990 301

Chapter 10: 1991-1992 323

Bibliography 330

Index by Manufacturer 331

Index by Location 333

Preface

The majority of fire apparatus in the United States are mounted on commercial chassis, and we thought that they deserved a book of their own. Also, we wanted to recognize the many firms and individual efforts that went into outfitting these chassis. Because many of the rigs described in this book tend to be operated by volunteers, we incorporated some descriptions of the volunteers' important roles in preventing and fighting fires.

We would like to acknowledge the help of the following: Bob Barraclough, Span Instruments; Jim Carney, National Truck Equipment Association; Ernest N. Day, New Jersey Fire Equipment Corporation; Oakley Dexter; David J. Gitchell, W.S. Darley & Co.; Ronda Robeson Guile, LaMesa Sheet Metal Works Inc.; John Gunnell, Old Cars Weekly News & Marketplace; Jim Johnson, Pierce Manufacturing Inc.; George L. Kanugh, Pierce Manufacturing Inc.; Dan Lew, San Francisco State University; Daniel Luethi, 3D Manufacturing Inc.; Tom MacGugan; Tom Nowak, Federal Signal Corporation; Edward A. Rash, Hannay Reels; Glen R. Vanderspiegel, Baker Equipment Engineering; and Tamara Wood. We give special thanks to Gene Olson and Bill West for their support.

Donald F. Wood
San Francisco State University
Wayne Sorensen
San Jose State University
December 1992

AMERICAN VOLUNTEER
FIRE TRUCKS

By Donald F. Wood
& Wayne Sorensen

Dedication

To Doreen and Charlotte

©1993 by

Donald F. Wood and Wayne Sorensen

Published by

**krause
publications**

700 E. State Street • Iola, WI 54990-0001

Library of Congress Catalog Number: 92-74800
ISBN: 0-87341-236-2
Printed in the United States of America

Introduction

FIRST STAGE: Bucket Brigades

The first stage of fire fighting in America was the "bucket brigade," so-called because the earliest equipment for fighting fire in the American Colonies was the leather fire bucket. In Boston and other cities, a watchman would give the alarm and the call would go out: "Throw out your buckets!" Most villages and towns required each household to supply a certain quota of buckets.

Two human lines were formed between the burning structure and the water source; one line passed the buckets of water to the fire, while the other line returned the empty buckets to be refilled at the water source. This was known as the bucket brigade. After the building had burned to the ground (known as "saving the lot") or the fire was put out, the buckets were piled in front of the town hall or meeting house, and each householder would call for his marked buckets.

On Oct. 4, 1948, a three-cent postage stamp was issued honoring volunteer firemen. The stamp showed a portrait of Benjamin Franklin, chief of the Union Fire Company of Philadelphia, said to be the first volunteer fire company in the American Colonies. The stamp also pictured a hand-pumping engine and a motorized pumping engine resembling a Mack "L" series pumper manufactured between 1940-1956.

Peter Stuyvesant, the one-legged Dutch governor of New Amsterdam, organized early fire protection efforts in his community. In 1648, he appointed fire wardens to enforce the fire laws. Wooden chimneys were forbidden. Money from fines was used to purchase buckets, hooks and ladders. Hooks were used to pull down frame walls to prevent fires from spreading. Each house paid a tax in order to raise funds to purchase leather buckets. In New Amsterdam, another early group of American firemen, the Prowlers, were assigned to patrol the streets from dusk until dawn. Their equipment was buckets and ladders.

The most prominent members of the community volunteered for fire duty to set the example for the rest of the citizens. George Washington served as a volunteer fireman in Alexandria, Virginia, and later, during his military and political trips, he visited fire companies in cities and towns, inspecting the local apparatus. Other leading citizens taking an active part in volunteer fire fighting were John Hancock, John Adams, and Paul Revere.

Early Fire Engines

Among the first fire engines to arrive in the Colonies was one that came to Boston in 1679. This was a wooden hand pumper imported from England. The first piece of fire apparatus made in the colonies is said to have been a hand pump by Thomas Lote. It was a copy of an English model known as the "Newsham." As towns became larger and wealthier, fire engines were purchased from England.

Philadelphia had a fire engine built in America by Abraham Bickley, but hand engines made by Richard Newsham were preferred by the American Colonies. The Newsham engine, patented in 1725, was the first hand engine to throw a continuous stream of water. The Newsham engine was a double-cylinder engine with an air chamber, suction pipe and a gooseneck nozzle.

A Philadelphia pump builder, Richard Mason, introduced end-levers on hand pumpers. Hand pumping was hard work requiring a large number of volunteers. One group would operate the pump handles while a second group stood behind them, resting and waiting to relieve them. Some pumpers had two levels of men at work with a second level standing on a narrow frame operating a second, higher level of handles. Such a pumper might use 30-plus men pumping with an equal number ready to relieve them.

The capabilities of hand engines progressed, and with the addition of suction enabling the engines to draft water directly from the source, there came the need for new equipment to carry more hose. Leather riveted fire hose had been developed in Philadelphia in 1808 by Sellers and Pennock. This was the standard fire hose throughout the United States until 1870, when rubber-lined cotton hose came into use. Simple four-wheel, hand-drawn hose wagons were developed to carry the hose. Companies added a bell, which soon became part of the fire fighting experience. A two-wheeled hose cart was developed to cope with unpaved streets. About 1808, the "jumper" hand-drawn hose cart, sometimes called a tender, was developed. An arched spring carriage was then developed to make handling easier on unpaved streets, and this evolved into hose carriages that were sometimes elaborately decorated.

William C. Hunneman of Boston, Massachusetts, an apprentice of Paul Revere, built hundreds of hand engines for volunteer fire companies in America and around the globe. This company had the reputation of building the best hand-pump fire engines, hose reels and ladder trucks. The end of the Hunneman line came in 1907, after having built 716 hand fire engines and 29 steam fire engines.

In 1834, two brothers, Lysander and Theodore Button, formed the L. Button Fire Engine Company to build hand engines. Other builders were: William Jeffers, Rumsey & Company, Sisly Manufacturing Company, and James Smith. A catalog published by the LaFrance Fire Engine Company of Elmira, New York listed hand fire engines manufactured in five sizes. Many manufacturers just built one hand engine and were in business only a few years. Hand engines and hose reels were built by carriage makers, machinists and blacksmiths in communities throughout the United States.

In about 1870, chemical engines were developed to fight small fires. They worked on the principle of reaction between an acid and a base: acid was added to a container of water and soda, and the reaction generated foam. These engines were popular with volunteers. Among the merits of a chemical engine is that it got into service quickly. However, the chemical engine was not designed for, nor was it capable of coping with, a large conflagration.

As cities and their structures grew, volunteers needed a way to transport ladders and hooks. Hand-drawn ladder trucks were introduced in Philadelphia in 1799. Later a tiller was added to the rear axle to help the truck turn at corners.

Transporting Water

Early methods of transporting water to the fire was hard and time-consuming work. Bucket brigades applied water directly on the fire and later furnished water for the hand engines. About 1796 bucket brigades started becoming obsolete with the development of wooden water mains in Boston. Then pumping stations were developed, and cast iron pipes enabled fire companies to take water from hydrants.

The water system in Philadelphia was the most successful of the early attempts and delivered a good supply of water piped from the Schuylkill River. It began its operations in 1801 and supplied 63 houses and four breweries, and was fitted with 37 fireplugs with pressure to meet the needs of the fire department. What is now known as the Liberty Bell was even used as a fire bell, summoning volunteers.

Water became critically scarce as cities grew, and water supplies were provided for consumptive uses as well as for fire fighting.

The Age of Volunteers

The first hundred years of fire fighting in the United States was definitely the age of the volunteer. In communities, the volunteer fire department organization was well organized. Each company elected its own officers and selected its own members. America had a militia of citizens involved in the volunteer fire companies.

Soldiers who returned from the Revolutionary War found volunteer companies carried on some of the excitement and comradeship of army life. Fire companies of the post-Revolution period filled the social void that war veterans' organizations filled at other times. The life of the volunteer was full of glamour, and engine companies had long lists of young men waiting for the limited openings. Volunteer firemen were a courageous, hard-working, self-sacrificing, colorful group of citizens. Disputes between rival companies were common and lawless behavior not unknown.

With end of the Revolutionary War, American firemen entered a new age, at least in big cities. Boston, New York, Philadelphia and other towns began to depend less on the inhabitants and their buckets and more on appointed fire fighters with their engines, hose, and knowledge. They experimented with longer streams and learned just what was the best pace to pump water. During this period, men began to bunk in at the firehouse for the night so they could make a quick response to an alarm. The first professional fire department in the United States was organized in Cincinnati on April 1, 1853.

SECOND STAGE: Steam and Horses

Hand-operated fire engines manned by volunteers required excessive manpower to operate their pumps, and they could not produce a steady stream that reached the tops of the taller buildings being built. Hand-operated pumps gave way to steam fire engines, and the latter became a symbol of dependability.

The first steam fire engines were developed in England, adopting a portable pumping engine run by steam to pump water out of the mines. The fire-fighting application of water pumps was easily grasped. However, volunteer fire companies in the United States considered the steam fire engine to be a challenge and threat to their lifestyle. They felt the steam fire engine would put an end to their rivalries, their roughness, their heroism, their parades and their pride. Volunteers were afraid of losing their prestige.

The second stage of fire fighting in America was the age of steam and horses. This system required paid fire fighters to tend to the horse and keep a small fire burning in the steamer. Alarm systems were developed during this age. Within cities with paid departments, disciplined organizations were formed and attempted to develop a spirit of "professionalism" with the chief sometimes carrying the title "chief engineer."

However, in smaller communities, volunteer fire companies still existed. Some had hand-drawn hand engines. Mostly, the equipment of the volunteer of this period was hand-drawn hose reels, ladder trucks, and chemical engines. The use of horses, like the use of steam engines, was laughed at by the volunteers. The volunteers looked on the use of steam and horses as an insult to their many strengths and virtues.

Fighting Fire in the West

Volunteer organizations were also forming in the West. Consider, for a moment, the volunteer fire fighters in Nevada City, California, on the edge of the Sierra, who have a long record of accomplishments. During the period from 1849 to 1860, fires were the least of anyone's worries in this roaring mining town. The miner worked in his grubby clothes, his tools were at the mine, and any gold he had was buried. It didn't take much to replace his shack.

Nevada City experienced three major fires, with the fire of 1856 almost burning the entire town to the ground and ruining many of its prosperous citizens. There was plenty of gold in the hills and the town was rebuilt. There was some talk of a fire department but the interest in the project fizzled, and no fire department was organized. It took two more large fires to bring a fire department into existence.

In May 23, 1858 200 buildings were lost. Thirty brick buildings withstood the fire, including the new courthouse and the stylish National Hotel. The women of Nevada City gave a ball on Dec. 26, 1859, and a week later they gave a theatrical show. Both events raised money towards the formation of a fire department. The "Mainstreeters" and the "Broadstreeters" wanted the headquarters of the fire department to be located in their part of the hilly town. The state law allowed one fire company to each 1000 people. Three rival fire companies were formed within 10 days, each reluctant to help the others in case of fire.

The Mainstreeters became the Nevada Hose Company No. 1, and were organized on June 12, 1860. (Today, their original building is occupied by the Nevada County Museum.) The Broadstreeters followed with the organization of the Eureka Hose Company No. 2. The Broadstreeters purchased a lot near the head of Broad Street and built the first permanent firehouse in Nevada City. (This firehouse is still in service, housing the fire department's rescue squad.) The third company, the Protection Hook & Ladder Company No. 1, did not last long: Its equipment was sold and the members joined the other companies. Eventually all three departments were consolidated, and the Nevada City Fire Department was organized.

On July 23, 1860, the Eureka Hose Company purchased a slightly used horse-drawn hose wagon from San Francisco's Pennsylvania Engine Company No. 12. This was a four-wheel wagon with gold-leaf letters, exclaiming "Pennsylvania Engine Co., No. 12." The Eureka Hose Company's members felt it would not be right to paint out the name on the wagon, so the volunteers changed their name from the Eureka Hose Company to Pennsylvania Engine Company. The number "1" of the numeral 12 was painted out. This change took place on Aug. 5, 1860, and the Pennsylvania Engine Company No. 2 came into existence. (This hose wagon still belongs to the department and is used in parades.)

A reservoir on Buckeye Hill was built and two miles of pipe (10-inch, six-inch, and four-inch), plus 28 hydrants, were installed. By June 1861, Nevada City was well supplied with water to fight fires.

Much later, on May 23, 1885, the water system failed when Nevada City had another disastrous fire. The pipelines clogged with mud from the silt in the reservoir. The volunteers called an angry protest meeting and threatened to resign unless they could get control of the water system. The Nevada City volunteers, along with fire fighters elsewhere, insisted that an adequate water supply was -- and is -- as necessary as volunteers and their equipment.

In Pocatello, Idaho, the initial volunteer effort was provided in the 1880s by employees of the Oregon Short Line Railroad, who kept a hand-drawn hose cart in a red shack near the railroad watchman's shanty. Water supplies were meager and response time great, especially when the hose cart got bogged down in the mud and had to be freed with shovels. Several major fires served a positive function only in the sense that they demonstrated the inadequacies of the volunteers, their equipment, and the town's water supply.

In 1894, the frustrated volunteers organized a meeting to explain to property owners that insurance rates were going to rise because of the town's inability to fight fires. However, no major business or property owners appeared or showed interest, and the volunteers decided to disband. In 1899, the Pocatello Opera House, one of the young community's most prominent buildings, burned to the ground. The public, viewing the blaze, were openly critical of both the poorly trained volunteers and their inadequate equipment.

The fire service in the town of Los Gatos, California, near San Jose, had a less stormy start. Los Gatos had a proud tradition, which dated to the early days when the community was settled, of neighbor helping neighbor to combat fire. In 1886, the Los Gatos Fire Department was formed by town citizens who volunteered their services to the community as fire fighters. Wooden construction and lack of adequate fire codes allowed periodic fires to devastate whole blocks of the business district as late as 1901. The hose and ladder companies did their best with hand-drawn hose carts and a ladder truck. The volunteer firemen were a dedicated group. When the Los Gatos fire bell sounded, they forgot about their business or profession and became firemen.

The Los Gatos fire bell has a history of its own. Cast of bronze, it weighed 2,500 pounds and served from 1899 until 1949. When installed on a 60-foot tower, it took the place of several church bells that had been rung to sound alarms. In its tower, the bell was rung by means of an electric striker, responding to alarms registered in one of six alarm boxes throughout the community.

In nearby Campbell, in 1898 when the Board of Trade was created, there were meager funds to meet the demands for fire protection. The town needed an abundant supply of water because water faucets and horse-watering troughs were not enough. The existing fire equipment consisted of 200 feet of two-inch cotton hose, a water cart, galvanized pails, two ladders and a few dollars in the bank. There was an outstanding bill of $14 for the hose. The board paid this bill and purchased two fire hooks. An ad in the local paper requested that citizens leave the ladders belonging to the fire department in their places except in case of fire.

The beginnings of the Yakima, Washington Fire Department were also modest. A bucket brigade of volunteers was organized in the early 1880s. By the year 1889 the department had three pieces of equipment: an 1889 Clapp and Jones horse-drawn steamer that was shipped around the Horn, a hook-and-ladder truck, and a hand-drawn hose cart. Usually there were about 20 volunteers on call, but in an emergency any passerby might be drafted into service at a fire.

THIRD STAGE: Motorized Fire Apparatus

It is at this juncture that we start our book. Larger communities had paid departments operating horse-drawn steamers while smaller communities were still running smaller equipment, often still hand-drawn and hand-operated. In terms of calendar time, we're at the beginning of the 20th century. The major development at this time was the gasoline-powered automobile, which -- in broad terms -- would transform the American society and the American landscape. In a narrower sense, the gasoline engine would have many impacts on both fire apparatus and the organization of personnel operating the apparatus. Thus, the third stage of fire fighting in the United States is that of motorized fire apparatus.

All fire departments started to study the practicality of motorized apparatus. Adaptive hitching equipment was developed so that trucks and truck-tractors could be placed at the front of rigs, literally taking the place of horses. Equipment on the chemical engines, usually two large chemical tanks and a hose reel, was placed on regular automobile or truck chassis because trucks could reach fires faster than horses. Auto and truck chassis were also used to carry hose wagon and ladder bodies. A major development was the ability to use the truck's gasoline engine to both propel the truck to the fire, and then to drive the pump. (Interestingly, in the early years of the century there was a development utilizing gasoline engine-powered pumps on horse-drawn wagons. These functioned the same as steam pumpers but could be operated cold, rather than requiring a fire to be maintained at all times to keep steam pressure. They were of value to volunteer departments since the pump did not require continual attention. However, as a development they were soon superceded by apparatus that used the gasoline engine for propulsion and then both propulsion and pumping.)

Existing pump and ladder apparatus builders, such as American LaFrance, Seagrave, Ahrens-Fox and Pirsch, developed their own motor truck chassis and, usually, the power train for their rigs. (In this book, these rigs will be referred to as "custom.") However, these custom apparatus builders had excess plant capacity and soon found that they could earn additional income by supplying their pumps and related equipment -- which had a fine reputation for quality -- on lower-cost, mass-produced makes of truck chassis. The truck chassis (and sometimes auto chassis) were referred to as commercial chassis and consisted of the wheels mounted on the frame, the engine and transmission, front fenders, hood, cowl, and sometimes even the cab. This chassis was shipped to an apparatus outfitter who finished and equipped it into a complete piece of fire apparatus, ready to go. The distinctions between custom apparatus and that on commercial chassis will be discussed later, although in this book we will emphasize the commercial chassis used in the fire service.

The volunteer in this third stage of fire fighting was and is an active, physically able, civic-minded member of his community. He or she leaves work, bed, or meal to respond to an alarm. One woman, whose father was a volunteer fire fighter, remembered:

"The town siren was a broad foghorn call that rose and fell in a long ululation, like the call of a bird. We could hear it anywhere in town, everyone could, and if I was away from our house I could run to the station. (I had to race the cars and pickups of other volunteer firemen, other teachers, and the butcher, the undertaker, an editor from the local newspaper, grinding out of parking lots and driveways all over town in a hail of pebbles.) If I was quick enough and lucky enough, I could stand to one side and watch the flat doors fly up, the trucks pull out one after the other covered with clinging men, and see my father driving by. He drove a short, stout pumper, and I waved and called to him high above my head. He never noticed

I was there, not once; it was as though he ceased to be my father when he was a fireman. The whistle of the siren was the whistle of another life, and he would disappear around a corner, face pursed with concentration, and be gone."[1]

Today's apparatus is well-equipped with the latest fire fighting tools, and today's volunteer knows how to use this equipment. Air tanks are almost always worn while inside a burning structure. Training is important to both the fire fighter and his fellow fighters since they are dependent upon each other. Many of today's fire fighters are also trained as paramedics. Two-way radios on apparatus keep the fire fighters in touch with headquarters and speed up the turnout and response to alarms. The volunteer is often called by radio beeper to respond to the alarm.

Being a volunteer fire fighter has social advantages. In many communities it is still a "rite of passage" for young men. And, in recent years, fire departments, both paid and volunteer, have also added women to their ranks. Having a volunteer fire department also says something about the community. "The presence of a firehouse in one's village was not to be scorned. Besides assuring residents a measure of protection, it attested to their organizing talents and to their resolve as a community to challenge disaster. Thus in poorer rural communities a volunteer fire company can be a metaphor for group achievement, a mark of municipal upward mobility."[2]

Even when the old-time volunteer fighters in the cities were replaced by paid departments, that was not the last of the volunteers. In many communities with paid departments, there is a back-up of volunteers available to respond to second alarms. There are many variations of paid and unpaid fire fighters. A small community might be able to pay only for a driver to be on duty at all times. When the alarm sounds, he drives the engine to the fire, slowing along the route to pick up a few volunteers along the way. In some traditional suburban communities with many residents working "downtown," there are more paid fire fighters on duty in the suburbs during the day, and fewer at night and on weekends when more volunteers are at home. In many departments, volunteers are paid small amounts for responding to fires. In industrial plants, refineries, or large institutions, workers either volunteer or are assigned to respond to fires on their grounds.

Just as there are all sorts of volunteers, there are also all sorts of equipment that they use. The next section will introduce that topic.

Types of Equipment

All the early motorized fire apparatus types evolved from horse-drawn and hand-drawn rigs.

Chemical cars consisted of one or two large, soda-acid type extinguishers with a hose reel. The soda mixture in one tank would be activated by adding acid, and the tank's contents would discharge through the hose. The second tank would then be activated while the first one was recharged. The operator would need additional quantities of soda and acid to continue charging the tanks as well as a supply of water. Probably the most common initial motorized rig in America's volunteer departments would be a Ford Model T carrying twin chemical tanks. Chemical tanks were also placed on hose wagons, pumpers, and ladder trucks, more specialized types of apparatus.

In larger cities, hose wagons were used in conjunction with pumpers. Early hose carts were merely a large hose reel mounted between two large wheels and pulled by men or, later, by horses. Large wheels were necessary for use on rough pavement. Four-wheel wagons, again either hand- or horse-drawn, were also used. The hose wagon driver would position it near the fire, while the pumper would be positioned near the hydrant.

Pumpers were also common and have evolved into the most widely used piece of equipment today. Hand pumpers were used until early in this century, and horse-drawn steam pumpers were used in city departments until about the time of World War I. Pumpers do require a regular and adequate water supply, and in many communities the provision of a dependable water supply was an important step in developing fire fighting capability. If there was sufficient pressure, the fire fighters would run their hoses directly

1. Sallie Tisdale, "Bound Upon a Wheel of Fire," **Harper's Magazine** (January 1990), page 77.
2. Richard J. Margolis, "For Volunteers, Dousing Flames is Only Part of the Job," **Smithsonian** (November 1983), page 159.

from the street hydrants to the fire, relying on the pumper only if they needed more pressure. In the 1920s, as pumpers evolved, the chemical tanks were replaced by "booster" tanks of water, pumped by using the truck's motor and discharging through a small diameter hose.

Where hydrants and other water supplies are unavailable, different strategies or equipment are used. Tankers are fire apparatus with large tanks. Today, some tankers also carry a large, portable tank, much like a swimming pool, that they assemble quickly at the fire site. They then discharge their tank's contents into the portable tank and drive off to the nearest hydrant or surface water source and take on another load of water.

"Brush" rigs are used for fighting wildland fires. Because of this, they are often equipped for off-road operation and, while they carry some water, they carry supplies of hand tools such as picks and shovels to be used by a large number of fire fighters working on fire lines.

Ladder trucks carry an assortment of ladders and specialized rescue tools. These were sometimes called city service trucks. Aerial ladders have one ladder that is raised by mechanical or hydraulic means. Snorkels have an elevated fire-fighting platform and, in some situations, are more maneuverable than aerial ladder trucks. Variations of aerial ladders and towers are continually being developed. The vast majority of volunteer departments do not have specialized ladder trucks because there are few structures in their jurisdictions that are that tall.

Today's rigs are still categorized by the number of different fire-fighting functions they perform. A "triple combination" pumper, sometimes referred to as "pumper" in the captions used in this book, carries a pump, 1-1/2-inch or greater diameter hose, larger diameter hose to connect with hydrants, suction hose to take water from streams, booster tank and booster hose reel, ground ladders, and a variety of other fire-fighting equipment such as axes, nozzles, lanterns, and crowbars. The majority of apparatus pictured in this book falls into this category. (Purists believe that only a pumper can be called a fire engine, and we will try to follow that convention.)

A quad carries all the equipment mentioned in the previous paragraph, plus a complement of long ground ladders. A quint has everything a quad carries, plus an aerial ladder.

Some fire departments operate rescue squads, which are usually trucks carrying an extensive assortment of equipment needed to rescue people from fires, natural disasters, or accidents. Today, one also sees paramedic vehicles and ambulances operated by volunteer departments.

Chassis and Apparatus Builders

Another way to categorize fire apparatus deals with whether it appears on a commercial chassis or is custom-made. Commercial chassis are those made by truck makers such as Chevrolet, Ford, and GMC. The chassis usually consists of the frame, wheels, power train, and sheet metal back to the cowl, sometimes including the enclosed cab. This chassis is shipped to an apparatus outfitter, such as Pierce, where a pump is installed along with a booster tank. Then a hose body is added along with racks for ladders, tool compartments and additional lights. The truck's make is still distinguishable as being a Chevrolet, Ford or GMC. We have, for purposes of simplification, assumed that nearly all volunteer rigs fit into this category. In reality, volunteer departments do run custom rigs. Wealthy communities sometimes buy custom rigs as a sign of appreciation of their volunteers who serve without pay. Sometimes, as a custom rig is retired from service with a full-time department, it is sold or donated to a neighboring volunteer department.

Many full-time departments use apparatus mounted on commercial chassis. In a few instances we have included pictures of these because they illustrate the usefulness of the commercial truck chassis. Interestingly, the same long commercial truck chassis developed for school bus bodies was also used to build ladder trucks for fire fighters.

In the United States, there have been nearly 2000 different makes, or marques, of trucks manufactured. The number is even greater when one remembers that most makes of autos were also available as light trucks. Today, only about a dozen makes remain, although to this could be added names of some foreign imports. However, relatively few foreign makes of trucks are used for mounting fire apparatus used in the United States.

We mentioned that the chassis was shipped to an apparatus outfitter for finishing. We would guess that there were hundreds of firms that were in the regular business of outfitting fire apparatus on commercial chassis. Many of these firms were truck body builders, and their fire engine line was but one of their offerings. They reached truck dealers with their catalogs and offered to work with the dealer in preparing his proposal to respond to the community's request for bids for new apparatus. Chevrolet dealers, for example, each year receive a Silver Book, which includes ads from truck body builders as well as suppliers of other equipment, such as all-wheel drive units or winches that can be mounted on a new truck. In the 1947 Silver Book there were full-page ads from six apparatus outfitters: American Fire Apparatus Company of Battle Creek, Michigan; Central Fire Truck Corporation of St. Louis; W.S. Darley of Chicago; H.O. DeBoer and Associates of Logansport, Indiana (which distributed Boyer apparatus); General Fire Truck Company of Detroit; and Howe Fire Apparatus of Anderson, Indiana. The 1954 Silver Book also had ads from six companies: Central; Darley; General; Howe; plus two that were not in the 1947 book. These two were W.J. Thiele of Johnstown, Pennsylvania, which featured rigs with special fog nozzles, and American LaFrance, probably the nation's best-known apparatus builder at that time. The American LaFrance ad had this message for the Chevrolet truck dealer:

"Our sales representative will co-operate with you. The chassis is to be delivered to our factory at Elmira, N.Y. where the complete equipment is installed and tested. We make delivery and furnish test engineer to run acceptance test in co-operation with State Rating Bureau Engineer. We also instruct the fire department personnel in correct operation."

Fire apparatus were also built by people in each community. Sometimes the volunteer fire fighters did most of the work themselves. Components could be purchased out of catalogs and mounted in a local blacksmith or body shop. It was not even necessary for the chassis to be new. A used rig could be utilized: Used petroleum or milk tank trucks were likely candidates since the tank was an important piece of equipment already in place. We estimate that thousands of rigs used by volunteer departments were built or outfitted on a one-time "one-of-a-kind" basis in local shops, garages, and fire stations throughout the country. The W.S. Darley Company deserves mention here since they published (and continue to publish) catalogs of supplies and equipment needed by municipalities. Starting in the late 1920s, their catalogs began including more and more items needed to construct and fully equip a "do-it-yourself" fire truck.

Custom rigs were built from the ground up by manufacturers whose names stood for fire-fighting excellence: American LaFrance, Ahrens-Fox, Maxim, Pirsch, and Seagrave. These were higher quality -- and much more expensive -- than units built on commercial chassis. However, nearly all custom rig manufacturers also outfitted commercial chassis. Here's one apparatus manufacturer's description of the differences between custom and commercial apparatus. It appeared in a Ward La France report in the early 1970s.

"Fire trucks are normally produced in two basic styles, commercial and custom. Commercial trucks are less expensive than the custom type, but are limited in features. For the production of a commercial truck, the manufacturer purchases the chassis, complete drive train and cab from a major truck producer such as Ford, GMC, Dodge or International. The pump is installed: the tank and rear body sections are fabricated and mounted on the purchased chassis. A limited number of options are available as to engine size, pump capacity and tank size.

"A custom vehicle is built completely to the customer's specifications. Such vehicles are normally more expensive than commercial vehicles and usually more profitable to manufacture and sell."

Some mention was found of custom manufacturers having some commercial rigs "in stock," meaning that the community would have the option of buying a new rig "off the rack." These rigs were probably built on speculation when the assembly lines were not very busy filling orders.

The number of custom manufacturers is quite small. In another book, dealing with apparatus from 1900 to 1960, we identified 18 makers of custom apparatus as having a nationwide presence: Ahrens-Fox, American LaFrance, Buffalo, Christie, Darley, FWD, Hale, Howe, Knox and Knox-Martin, Mack, Maxim, Pirsch, Seagrave, Stutz, U.S.A., Ward LaFrance, and Webb; and nearly all of these outfitted commercial chassis as well. Only five or six on that list of 18 survive to this day.

Some truck manufacturers were in both markets: They provided chassis to other outfitters and also built and sold their own line of apparatus mounted on their own chassis. Mack was the best-known example although it dropped out of the custom market about a decade ago. Both International and White also marketed their own lines decades ago. For that matter, a few custom fire apparatus manufacturers also built and sold commercial trucks, the best-known examples being American LaFrance and Ward LaFrance. There are also a few truck manufacturers with names that are not widely known who build very large specialized chassis that are then outfitted with large bodies as, say, cement mixers, cranes, or refuse haulers. Some of these chassis are also used for "custom" fire-fighting rigs.

We do have a brief glimpse of the market as it existed a generation ago. Ward LaFrance estimated that of the 3555 pieces of new fire apparatus sold in the United States in 1971, just under half (48 percent) were commercial pumpers, while about one third (30 percent) were custom pumpers. The average price then for a commercial pumper was $21,388 and for a custom pumper, $43,479. Ladder trucks accounted for less than eight percent of the units sold; and nearly all of them were custom, with the average cost that year for a custom tractor-drawn aerial being $83,685. The same report indicated that there were 25,000 fire departments in the United States, 18,000 volunteers and 7000 paid.

This book consists of 10 chapters, one for each decade in the 20th century. We have tried to present as wide a range of chassis builders and apparatus outfitters as space allowed. In picture captions, the term "Reo/Seagrave" means a Reo chassis that Seagrave completed into a fully functional fire engine. We pay special attention to "homemade" rigs because, while they usually were not very stylish, they demonstrate still more facets of volunteer fire fighters' abilities and contributions to their communities.

First Permanent Firehouse of the Nevada City Volunteer Fire Department. Credit: Nevada County Historical Society.

The House of Pennsylvania Engine Co. No. 2. The cornerstone laid with impressive ceremonies on Oct. 17, 1860, and the building was finished and occupied Jan. 14, 1881. Located on upper Broad Street, Nevada City, California, the building is still in use by the fire department, housing the rescue squad. Credit: Wayne Sorensen Collection.

Volunteers in New Glarus, Wisconsin show how a ladder rig was once pulled by volunteers wearing chest harnesses. Credit: Walt Schryver.

This hand engine dates from 1820 when it was used by volunteers in New York City. Then, it was shipped around the Horn through the Golden Gate in 1850 to serve as San Francisco's engine 1. In about 1854 the Empire Engine Company of San Jose purchased the rig. It was restored in 1975 by the Sierra Conservation Center. Large numbers of volunteers were required to operate the rig at a fire. In addition to those working the pump, an equal number would be standing behind them, waiting to take their places as they needed rest. In addition, the unit was hand-drawn. Credit: Wayne Sorensen Collection.

This early hose cart was pulled by hand. Five-foot wheels were needed for rough streets. It was built by Gleason & Bailey of Seneca Falls, New York. Credit: Wayne Sorensen Collection.

This photo shows the large number of men needed to pump a hand unit and shows the height of the stream it can throw. The muster was held in July 1962 and shows the winning stream of Protection No. 1 of Newbury, Massachusetts (222 feet). The Protection was built in 1865 by the Jeffers Company. Credit: Fitchburg Sentinel.

Cowing and Company of Seneca Falls, New York built hand engines from about 1853 to 1868. In 1889, Sellersville, Pennsylvania purchased this 1861 hand fire engine from Bethlehem, Pennsylvania. It is shown drafting. The suction hose was permanently attached to the rear of the engine, and when not in use was swung up over the top and held in place by a large brass pipe. Credit: Wayne Sorensen Collection.

This hand-drawn chemical rig was built by Chas. T. Holloway & Company. To the front of the front axle are two reels for rope to be used by the volunteers as they pulled the rig. It also has a hose reel, some lanterns, and a hand-held extinguisher. Credit: Chas. T. Holloway & Company.

Rumsey and Company of Seneca Falls, New York, built this light village hook and ladder truck. Today, we'd say that it was a "labor-intensive" piece of equipment since it was drawn by hand, the ladders were raised by hand, and the buckets required a chain of volunteers stretching from the water source to the fire. Credit: Rumsey.

A 1865 Silsby rotary gear steam fire engine, which was hand-drawn, was originally built for San Francisco. It proved to be too heavy for hills and was then sold to Marysville, California. Credit: Wayne Sorensen Collection.

A Seagrave combination chemical and hose wagon used in Pocatello, Idaho. It was horse-drawn and there was a corral at the rear of the station for the horses. Pumps were not needed since hydrants had sufficient water pressure from reservoirs in nearby hills. This is one of two similar units; rail tracks split the town and it was necessary to have a station on each side. Credit: Bannock County Historical Museum Collection.

Chas. T. Holloway & Company built this double-cylinder, two-wheel Holloway Chemical Engine. It was drawn by hand or by one horse. Credit: Chas. T. Holloway & Company.

Shortly after 1874, Amaden, California installed a system of fire hydrants and constructed a bell tower with a hose cart. Credit: Forbes Mill Museum-Los Gatos, California.

A bell once was used to summon volunteers in Black River Falls, Wisconsin. It was replaced by a siren, and the volunteers now carry pagers. Credit: Don Wood.

20

Nevada City's volunteers responded to this fire horn mounted on the the bell tower. Credit: Ethlie Ann Vare.

A "crane neck" Cowing & Company pumper on a practice run in 1894 with about two dozen volunteers on the main street of Stayton, Oregon. The unit was originally sold to San Francisco in 1860. It was then sold to Albany, Oregon in about 1880 and, in 1888, was acquired by Stayton. Credit: Wayne Sorensen Collection.

Fire protection is a fundamental responsibility of government. Here in central Wisconsin we see a town hall with the fire station to the right. Credit: Don Wood.

Westinghouse Gasoline Fire Engine

Sizes—350 to 1000 Gallons Per Minute.

ENGINE: 4-Cylinders, Four Cycle.
IGNITION: Jump Spark Double Set—positive action.
COOLING: Uses water from main pump.
GASOLINE: Tank holds supply for one day run.
PUMP: Impeller type. Direct-driven.
HOSE FIXTURE: Convenient, Adjustable and Adaptable.
TRUCKS: Spring mounting front and rear and flexible.
BRAKE: Hub brake used when wheels rubber tired.
WEIGHT: Two-thirds of steam apparatus.
LOW CENTRE OF GRAVITY. Very portable. Maintain pressure.
STARTS and delivers water within ten seconds.
AUTOMATIC CONTROL for stopping pump when operating shut-off nozzles.

THE WESTINGHOUSE COMPANY
SCHENECTADY, N. Y.

Here's a hint of what the 20th century would bring. This is an ad for a horse-drawn Westinghouse gasoline fire engine at the turn of the century. A few of the advertised features show the advantages over steam engines: low center of gravity, less weight, and ability to start and deliver water within 12 seconds. Credit: Wayne Sorensen Collection.

Chapter 1
1901-1910

Trucks in this early era were little more than a motor built on to -- or under -- a wagon. Tires were of solid rubber, providing a hard ride. Gasoline engines were the most common power, although a few steam and electric rigs were used.

In Los Gatos, California, a fire in a livery stable in 1901 spread out of control and eventually burned the 60-foot wooden tower that carried the community's fire bell. The 2,500-pound bell, with a 12-foot circumference at the lip, fell and was cracked. It was still usable and hung again, this time in a steel tower, where it would serve well into the century. The Los Gatos fire bell had an Acme bell striking machine sold by the Gamewell Fire Alarm Telegraph Company of New York. (This firm was well known for its telegraphic fire alarm box systems. Bell striking machines were powered by the single winding of a weight that could produce 10,000 blows as it slowly lowered through a 21-foot drop. They were developed by Moses Crane, associated with Gamewell.) In neighboring Campbell, in 1904, the Board of Trade authorized the construction of a suitable house for fire equipment. By this time the town had seven fire hydrants.

By 1902, Pocatello owned a hose cart and a ladder truck, and this was supplemented by a hose cart owned by the Oregon Short Line Railroad. The city's department had 45 volunteers plus 15 who operated the railroad's rig. The community had 19 fire alarms and 28 hydrants, although muddy streets continued to hinder the movement of equipment, and sometimes there was not enough hose to reach from the water source to the fire. In 1910, the city purchased a horse-drawn Seagrave combination chemical and hose wagon for $1,800 and 1000 feet of hose for $900. Volunteers were paid $1 for their first hour at each response, and 50 cents per hour for additional time spent at the fire scene. Better equipment and training, as well as improvements in the water supply, brought insurance rates down.

Between fires in Yakima, Washington, the fire department had to fight the city council, which was stingy with funds. The few appropriations were augmented by proceeds of an annual firemen's ball. There was a small payment to the volunteer for each fire he fought. Most of the time the city was slow to pay the volunteers, so, in 1904, the volunteers voted to disband. A new department was formed to include five paid firemen and 10 volunteers (call men). Turnover of the volunteers was frequent, and membership in the volunteers was easy to obtain. To be a volunteer one had to be at least 18 years old, a citizen and able to speak understandable English. There was a fee of $1 for initiation. The wages of the paid department were small and the hours long. Fire fighters were on duty at the firehouse 21 hours a day, six days a week, with time out for three meals which were eaten at home.

In 1906, the first motorized hose truck was purchased and placed into service. This is said to be the first motorized hose wagon west of the Mississippi and the first motorized apparatus in the state of Washington. The purchase was not made outright, but on the condition the city would pay for the truck provided it met the specifications set by the council. The purchase price was $2200 net.

In Coalinga, California, the city organized its volunteer fire department. Sections of the 1906 ordinance dealt with organizing and controlling the department, selecting the chief and the assistant chief, granting permission to the chief and assistant chief to order the destruction of buildings if necessary to prevent the spread of a fire, and assessing penalties for turning in false alarms, driving over hoses, or refusing to shut off private faucets after a fire alarm has sounded. In 1910, Coalinga added doors to its fire station, although some citizens thought that the purpose was to make the building into an a "fine all-weather boxing ring, Coalinga fire fighters' favorite pastime of the era."[1]

At the turn of the century there was as much interest in the development of electricity as there was in the internal combustion engine. An article in a 1910 issue of *Scientific American* proposed development of apparatus propelled by gasoline engines carrying electrically driven centrifugal pumps; and for electric power, one would tap into overhead trolley or other electric wire systems. These electric sources are "at almost every street corner and quite as well distributed as hydrants. The same condition also prevails in many rural districts where electric light and trolley lines are to be found on every main street."[2]

Some U.S. truck manufacturers, whose names we recognize today, got their start in this first decade of the century. Mack and White were formed about 1900. International Harvester, a well-known farm implement manufacturer, turned out its first truck, a high-wheeler, in 1905. Ransome E. Olds left Oldsmobile and formed a second company which turned out Reo autos and trucks. The first Autocars were built in 1908.

Ford autos were introduced during this early decade. Specific mention also should be made of the Ford Model T, introduced in 1908. Model Ts were turned out for nearly 20 years. They had great influence in reshaping the nation. Other manufacturers built kits one could use to convert early Model T autos into trucks. The kits converted the Ford's rear wheels into sprockets and linked them by chains to the new rear wheels on the extended frame.

At the end of 1910, there were only about 10,000 trucks and 19 million horses in the United States. There was interest in adapting the motor truck to many uses, including fire service. A 1910 magazine article about fire apparatus noted: "At present, motor apparatus is most widely used in suburbs and small cities with wooden dwellings, in other words, in communities where its high speed renders it possible to cover a much greater territory by a single company, and where infrequent alarms reduce the expense of maintenance far below that entailed in feeding and shoeing horses."[3] For this period, though, what motorized apparatus we see is either substituting a gasoline motor for horses in a horse-drawn body, or placing chemical tanks in an auto or light truck chassis. There was also substitution of a gasoline-driven pump for a steam pump on a horse-drawn body. There was limited development of rigs where the gasoline engine powered both the truck and the pump. Only in a few rigs could one see the lines of future apparatus.

1. *Oil But No Water, a History of the Coalinga Fire Department* (Coalinga, CA: the Fire Department, ca 1980), page 11.
2. Herbert T. Wade, "Automobile Fire Engines," *Scientific American* (Jan. 15, 1910), page 54.
3. Wade, page 54.

A number of gasoline-powered pumpers drawn by hand or horses were being sold by 1905. On the left is Richmond, Staten Island, New York's 1905 Waterous gasoline-powered pumper and on the right is Oakland, New Jersey's 1901 Howe gasoline pumper. Photo taken at a present-day muster. Credit: Ed Hass.

A 1910 Waterous single-cylinder gasoline pump pulled by oxen in Saskatoon, Saskatchewan. Credit: W.A. McDonnell.

Built by Auto Car Equipment Company of Buffalo, New York, this 1909 motor-propelled apparatus, the first motorized fire engine in New Jersey, contained the chemical equipment off an 1891 horse-drawn Holloway: two 60-gallon chemical tanks. It was delivered to Stokes Volunteer Fire Company of Ocean Grove, New Jersey. Credit: E.H. Stokes Fire Company, Ocean Grove, New Jersey.

A circa 1910 International chemical and hose rig used by the Marion Fire Department. Credit: Navistar Archives.

For a short period of time, between 1904 and 1907, Mercedes automobiles were manu-factured in Queens, New York. Initially the factory had been used to strengthen axles of German-built cars so that they could run on U.S. roads. In this era various Mercedes runabout and racing models were owned by society names such as Astor, Frick, Gould, Guggenheim, Vanderbilt, and Whitney. The runabouts were driven in Long Island and Newport, and raced in the winter in Florida. Shown here is a hose wagon mounted on an American-built 1905 Mercedes runabout. The runabout had been garaged at the estate of Mrs. Ida Beach Stewart where a fire occurred in 1914. In gratitude to the quick response by the Sea Cliff, New York fire department, Mrs. Stewart gave them this Mer-cedes, which they converted to a hose wagon and used it as a tractor to pull their department's Nott steamer. Credit: Incorporated Village of Sea Cliff, Nassau County, New York.

Knox trucks were built in Springfield, Massachusetts starting in 1901. This rig dates from about 1909 and, although not manned by volunteers, it shows the evolution from horse-drawn wagons to motorized apparatus. One could call it a motorized wagon. (Note fire fighters sitting on bench seats in rear. For nearly all of this century, fire fighters stood at the rear of rigs; but apparatus being built today must provide seats for everyone.)

The Pope Manufacturing Company of Hartford, Connecticut built motorized fire apparatus for a short time. This 1910 combination chemical and hose car went to Westfield, Massachusetts. Credit: Charles E. Beckwith.

Brantford, Ontario, Canada purchased this 1910 combination chemical and hose rig with a hand-cranked siren. It was built by Pope Hartford. Credit: A. Hardy.

Walter automobiles had some relationship to Walter trucks. This 1908 Walter commercial chassis carries a chemical tank. Credit: American Truck Historical Society.

This 1906 Waterous, used in Alameda, California, is a significant link in the development of motorized fire apparatus since it used the same engine to power its motion and its pump. Note that it carries only inlet hose, similar to steam pumpers of that era. Credit: Wayne Sorensen Collection.

This rig was used by salesmen of large chemical extinguishers. A two-tank unit is shown; it could be installed in a truck bed. Credit: Motor Vehicle Manufacturers Association.

Appearing to be top heavy, this 1910 White with right-hand steering carried a chemical tank, a reel of canvas hose, and several ladders. Firemen's helmets hang from ladder racks. Credit: Volvo/White.

Chapter 2
1911-1920

The second decade of this century was to be much more important in the development of trucks and their use for fighting fires. In the first part of the decade, tractors were still being sold to pull steam pumpers. By the decade's end, several builders of commercial chassis were well known nationwide.

The U.S. Army had been following these developments in trucks. In 1912, they sponsored a 1500-mile road test lasting nearly 50 days. The route stretched from Washington, D.C, via Atlanta, to Fort Benjamin Harrison, near Indianapolis. Three makes of trucks made the run: Autocar, FWD, and White. In 1916, when U.S. Army troops went into Mexico chasing Pancho Villa, the expedition was motorized. Pictures of the expedition show mostly Dodges and Whites.

World War I started in Europe in 1914. Even before the United States became involved directly, allied powers -- Britain, France, and Russia -- were purchasing trucks from United States manufacturers. In the early days of the war, horses were widely used at the front. As the war wore on, trucks began taking the place of horses. In 1917, the United States declared war on Germany, and our government placed large orders for trucks. A problem facing the Army was that there were a large number of different truck manufacturers. This would make it difficult to stock replacement parts. So the government drew up plans for a single truck, called the "Liberty" or the "USA." It was a sturdy truck and could carry three tons. A number of different manufacturers all built the same truck. In total, nearly 10,000 were produced.

World War I was an important training ground for truck drivers. Many had not driven a motor vehicle previously. The war demonstrated the truck's superiority over the horse. The war was also a testing ground for equipment. Trucks had to be rugged and dependable to survive in war.

Several well-known truck makes were introduced during this decade. GMC, Brockway, and FWD started in 1912. Hendrickson trucks were introduced in 1913. Dodge was formed in 1916, and built a screenside canopy truck. In 1917 Oshkosh Truck Corporation was formed. The first Chevrolet trucks were built in 1918.

During this entire decade, Ford Model T automobiles were very popular, and other manufacturers were building and selling kits to convert Model T auto chassis into trucks. The kits extended the wheelbase and strengthened the frame, and, initially, supplied solid rubber tires for the rear. Ford, recognizing the popularity of these kits, came out with a one-ton truck version of the Model T in 1917, known as the Ford Model TT. It sold for $600.

No doubt, the most significant single vehicle in the motorization of volunteer fire departments was the Model T or TT. When it was introduced in 1908, it was little more than a curiosity, and by the time its production runs ended in 1927, it was the most popular make of car or truck on the road. In this spread of two decades, both our society and economy changed, and the Model T was responsible for much of this change.

Ford dealers were in every community. Fords were cheap, dependable, and easy to find parts for. Because they were so common, many knew how to drive them. The most common fire-fighting apparatus mounted on the Ford Model T was a twin-tank chemical unit. This equipment usually consisted of two tanks linked to discharge through a single hose (kept on a reel or stored in a wire mesh basket). The equipment was easily mounted on the chassis and frame of the standard Ford roadster or touring chassis by volunteers doing the work themselves. The coupe's trunk or rear half of the touring car body was unbolted and removed. The fire-fighting body's sills were already drilled, ready to be bolted quickly to the frame. The result was a well-built, low-priced fire-fighting machine for the small town and village. Similar to the "attack pumpers" of today, the nimble Ford could be driven quickly to the fire scene by the first volunteers responding. In Campbell, California, a fire district was formed in 1918, and a Ford Model T outfitted by the American LaFrance Fire Engine Company was purchased. This was a double tank chemical rig that pulled a hose trailer. This was the first motorized fire-fighting vehicle owned by Campbell, and it served until 1937.

American LaFrance also supplied a combination chemical cars combined with a hose car body designed for mounting on the one-ton Ford Model TT or a comparable truck chassis. The equipment was furnished completely assembled, ready to be attached to the truck frame. When the body was bolted to the truck frame, the rig was ready for fire-fighting service. Again, volunteers could do the work, especially if they had some help from the local wagon builder or blacksmith.

There were other apparatus builders who equipped Ford Model Ts and TTs. During World War I, the Howe Fire Apparatus Company of Anderson, Indiana built more than 150 Ford Model T triple combination pumpers to protect military bases in the United States and France. At the time, it was considered the most efficient and economical unit on the market. These were built on an extended wheelbase Model T chassis with a two-passenger roadster type body in front.

Peter Pirsch & Sons Company of Kenosha, Wisconsin also designed combination chemical and hose body equipment for the Ford one-ton chassis. This could be adapted to other chassis. Pirsch also supplied a triple combination chemical hose pump body with equipment for any commercial chassis. The pump was of the rotary gear type. Other builders in this era who supplied chemical tanks that could be fitted to Ford Model Ts and other small chassis were: Barton, Obenchain-Boyer, and Waterous. Northern Fire Apparatus of Minneapolis ran an ad in an auto dealers' trade magazine with separate pictures showing a Nash, Dodge, Reo, FWD, and Pierce-Arrow, each equipped with Northern chemical tanks. A portion of the ad's text said: "Your chassis -- Northern-equipped -- makes a good fire truck. You can make big money selling this combination to towns in your territory. Over 250 dealers have made extra profits on such sales, selling over 25 different makes of chasses...."[1]

Trucks were replacing horses in fire stations during this decade. An article that appeared in 1918 concerning the volunteer fire department in Reading, Pennsylvania indicated that it operated 14 companies. Their roster of equipment included:

LaFrance triple pumping engines	2
Tractor-drawn steam engines	4
Horse-drawn steam engines	6
Motor aerial trucks	3
Chemical engine, motor	1
Chemical engine, horse-drawn	1
Auto combination chemical wagons	8
Horse-drawn chemical wagons	4 [2]

An accompanying article in the same magazine showed one more task that the motorized apparatus could perform: Fire fighters in Middletown, Connecticut developed a device that used a truck's exhaust to heat and thaw frozen hydrants.[3]

By 1913, Pocatello, Idaho had two horse-drawn chemical and hose wagons, plus a chief's buggy. There were two stations, one on each side of a major railroad line that split the community. The department had two paid and 24 volunteer fire fighters. Alarms were received by telephone and by a telegraph

1. *Automobile Trade Journal* (September 1918), page 262. Note that the ad spelled the plural of chassis as chasses; more recent usage has chassis stand for singular or plural.

2. *The American City* (October 1918), page 285. The Reading Volunteer Fire Department began in 1773.

3. *The American City* (October 1918), page 286. A two-inch pipe was connected to the exhaust of the truck and reduced down to three-quarters of an inch, and then was connected to a short hose. The hose was placed in the open, frozen hydrant.

system. The first impulse over the box system threw on the light switch inside the station and released the horses from their stall, ready to be harnessed. After major fires at the high school in 1914 and in the business district in 1915, Pocatello purchased a motorized American LaFrance combination pump and hose car (which exists today in the Bannock County Museum). Other motorized rigs were built on a Cadillac chassis and a White chassis, with the latter used to mount one of the formerly horse-drawn chemical and hose bodies.

Yakima, Washington purchased its second piece of motorized apparatus in 1911, a Knox double chemical tank and hose car that pulled their formerly horse-drawn steamer. In 1912, a 600-gpm Webb pumper was purchased, and in 1913 a gas-electric aerial was added. Each driving wheel was powered by an individual motor, and the individual motors were powered by a gasoline generator. The ladder cranked up by hand. Horses were retired from the department. Nevada City, California bought their first motor-driven fire truck, a 1913 Seagrave combination chemical and hose car. Their second motor-driven fire truck was a 1917 Brockway. The third motorized apparatus was built by the volunteers on the chassis of a Studebaker touring car with a front-mounted pump. In Los Gatos, California, three hose carts and a ladder wagon were the only fire equipment until 1915 when the first motorized apparatus was purchased, a 1915 American LaFrance type "40" combination chemical and hose car. In Davis, California, a volunteer fire department was formed in 1918, consisting of a chief, an assistant chief, and 15 members. Their first rig was a 1918 Studebaker with a 55-gallon soda and acid chemical tank, plus 200 feet of hose.

During this decade, trucks took on a more standardized appearance. They came with electric lights, and pneumatic tires were fairly common on fire apparatus by 1920. Trucks were also becoming relatively dependable. At the decade's end in 1920, about 322,000 new trucks and buses were sold. This was over 50 times the sales in 1910, when only 6,000 units were sold. In the year 1920, total truck and bus registrations in the United States exceeded one million units for the first time. There were about 200 different makes of trucks being manufactured at this time.

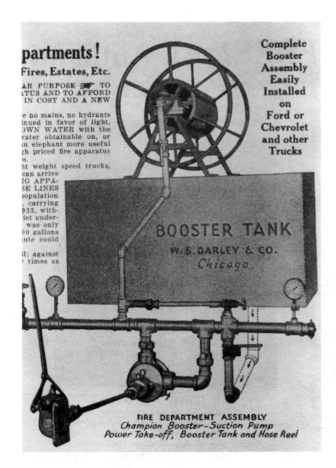

Early Darley catalogs advertised this booster tank, hose reel and pump unit that could be placed on homemade rigs. The pump was driven by the truck's power-takeoff. Credit: W.S. Darley.

This custom rig was a 1915 American LaFrance Type 40 combination hose and chemical car. It left the factory in Elmira, New York on Sept. 3, 1915. This rig had a four-cylinder, 75 hp engine and was equipped with two 35-gallon chemical tanks. This was Los Gatos, California's first motorized apparatus. The pneumatic tires exploded in a fire, and the volunteers had trouble moving the truck, so the volunteers decided to replace the pneumatic tires with hard rubber. Credit: Wayne Sorensen Collection.

A 1920 Atterbury combination chemical and hose car with solid tires and right-hand drive. Credit: Wayne Sorensen Collection.

The Robinson Fire Apparatus Manufacturing Company of St. Louis, Missouri used a Chadwick Great Six chassis to build a 750-gpm pumper for Wichita Falls, Texas. Credit: Wayne Sorensen Collection.

A Corbitt one-ton chassis, circa 1920, carrying a combination chemical and hose body. It ran on solid tires. Credit: American Truck Historical Society.

Waterloo, Iowa used a 1915 chassis built in their city (by Dart Motor Truck Company) for their chemical and hose car. Credit: Wayne Sorensen Collection.

Detroit Lakes, Minnesota used this two-tank chemical car mounted on a 1920 Dodge chassis. Men are bundled in warm clothing, and rear wheels have chains. Credit: Becker County Historical Society.

A 1914 Federal used in Tupelo, Mississippi. Credit: Motor Vehicle Manufacturers Association.

A 1917 Ford Model T chemical and hose combination built by Redwine Company of Mountain View, California, for Mountain View. The truck responded to its first alarm March 13, 1918, and is still used as a parade piece. (Some departments with Ford Model T parade pieces have trouble finding drivers today who know how to use the vehicle's pedals.) Credit: Wayne Sorensen Collection.

Campbell, California purchased this 1918 Ford Model T two-tank chemical with a four-wheel hose trailer. The rig was built by American LaFrance and sold for $1775. It was in service until 1937. Credit: Wayne Sorensen Collection.

The fire department in Healdsburg, California still uses this Ford Model T twin-tank chemical car in parades. Close-up shows working end of chemical tanks. Credit: Don Wood.

American LaFrance Type 32 two-tank chemical mounted on a 1919 Ford Model TT chassis for Homestead, Florida. Credit: American LaFrance.

Close-up of American LaFrance two-tank chemical body on a Ford Model TT owned by the Valley of the Moon, California fire department. Note screw-top cap on top of tank. When removed, the tank is filled with water/soda solution. Inside the top is a heavy metal cup, about twice the size of a coffee mug, into which acid is poured. The top is replaced and screwed tight. The operator would then press down on the lever that looks like a steering column gear shift lever, which would dump the acid into the soda. This side of the lever is a wheel that looks like a ship's wheel. It is attached to paddles inside the tank, used to agitate the mixture, furthering the chemical reaction. The foam would discharge through the hose. Credit: Don Wood.

A 1920 Ford Model T hose wagon built for volunteers in Santa Clara, California. Credit: Wayne Sorensen Collection.

A 1915 Franklin touring car built into a squad car for the Commercial Fire Dispatch of Berkeley, California, a firm run by insurance companies to protect policyholders' property from water and smoke damage during a fire. Credit: Wayne Sorensen Collection.

A late teens FWD with right-hand steering and chains on all four wheels, pulling a steam engine pump to a fire. Credit: FWD.

This originally was a 1915 FWD. Later, it was rebuilt and given a '30s appearance. Credit: American Truck Historical Society.

Northern Fire Apparatus Company of Minneapolis used a 1920 chassis built by Garford Motor Truck Company of Lima, Ohio to build a 350-gpm triple combination for Milford, Maine. It's shown pumping at a fire. Hood is raised for cooling. Credit: Lynn Sams.

The Fame Fire Company in Lewistown, Pennsylvania used this 1912 International high wheeler as a hose wagon. Note large warning gong in front. Credit: Wayne Sorensen Collection.

Several thousand different makes of trucks were manufactured in the United States, and a very common pattern was for the city where the truck was manufactured to use that make for its fire apparatus. Such was the case in Lima, Ohio where, in 1915, orders were placed for Gramm Bernstein chemical rigs, like the one pictured here. According to records of the Allen County Historical Society, the company lost $2000 in filling the order. Prices of materials had been escalating due to World War I, and the firm's bid had been too low. Credit: Allen County Historical Society.

Here's a 1916 International combination chemical and hose car, body work by Northern, pulling a Waterous gas trailer pump, which served Metropolis, Illinois. Credit: Wayne Sorensen Collection.

Two views of a circa 1918 International with a single chemical tank, bound for the Rapid City (South Dakota) Fire Department. Credit: Navistar Archives.

Kissel was a well-known maker of autos, which also built light truck and bus chassis. The firm was located in Hartford, Wisconsin. Here's a chemical body on a Kissel chassis, circa World War I, used by Stoughton, Wisconsin. Credit: The William F. Harrah Automobile Foundation.

In 1911, Knox Automobile Company of Springfield, Massachusetts built this combination chemical and hose car for Providence, Rhode Island. Knox was a pioneer in the motor fire apparatus field. Credit: Wayne Sorensen Collection.

A 1912 combination pumper, chemical and hose car built for West Haven, Connecticut by Knox Automobile Company. (We believe that the "1906" in left bottom is incorrect.) Credit: Wayne Sorensen Collection.

This 1912 Locomobile chassis was used as a tractor by the Goodwill Fire Company of Bridgeport, Pennsylvania to pull a horse-drawn city service semi-trailer. Credit: Wayne Sorensen Collection.

Wallace, Idaho's 1917 Mack AC hose wagon with snowplow blade. In the period prior to 1930, bus companies and motor carriers of freight often had to do their own snowplowing. Possibly this rig kept the streets cleared of snow so that it could respond to fires. Credit: Wayne Sorensen Collection.

A 1919 Mack AC city service ladder truck used in Long Branch, New Jersey. Helmets hang along the side. Credit: John J. Bobrecht.

The Maxwell-Briscoe Motor Company of Tarrytown, New York built the 1920 chassis for this Coffeyville, Kansas hose truck. Credit: Wayne Sorensen Collection.

A 1913 Model J Reo carrying double chemical tanks and a hose body was used by the Wanaque Valley volunteer fire company in New Jersey. Credit: Frank Malatesta.

Oakland, Iowa volunteer firemen are ready for action on their 1917 Reo chemical and hose car. Credit: Wayne Sorensen Collection.

This 1919 Reo chassis was outfitted by Pirsch to build a combination chemical and hose car for the Allis Chalmers Manufacturing Company of West Allis, Wisconsin. Plant workers were probably told to serve as needed. Credit: Dick Adelman.

Sauer trucks were built until just before World War I when their parent firm, International Motor Company, decided to concentrate on producing Macks. This rig is a Sauer from about 1914, being outfitted to fight fires. It has an overhead ladder rack, a large chemical tank and two hose reels. Credit: Mack Museum.

Here's a custom rig used by a volunteer department. Nevada City, California's first motorized apparatus left the Seagrave factory March 4, 1913. It had an air-cooled engine and was a combination chemical and hose car. Credit: Ron and Trish Packard.

Redwood City, California used this 1915 Schneer combination chemical and hose wagon that was rebuilt with pneumatic tires and disk-like wheels and booster tank. Schneer trucks were built in San Francisco. Credit: John Graham.

The Service Motor Truck Company of Wabash, Indiana built the chassis for Logansport, Indiana's two-tank chemical and hose car. Photo is from a factory brochure from about the time of World War I. Credit: Wabash County Historical Museum.

A 1912 Waterous gasoline-driven pumping engine used by the volunteer fire department in Iola, Wisconsin. At one time, the rig belonged to Chet Krause of Krause Publications, and it currently stands inside the entrance to Pierce Manufacturing Inc. of Appleton, Wisconsin - a well-known present-day apparatus manufacturer. Credit: Don Wood.

Webb Motor Fire Apparatus Company built this combination pump and hose car on a 1914 Thomas automobile chassis for Youngstown, Ohio. Credit: Wayne Sorensen Collection.

A 1913 White combination chemical and hose car built for Lawton, Oklahoma. For a period of time, White marketed its own line of fire-fighting apparatus. Credit: White Motor Company.

These four White triple combinations were ordered by the War Department during World War I. Two went to Camp Gordon, Georgia and two went to Camp Travis, Texas. Credit: Volvo/White.

This 1918 White, a 350-gpm triple combination, was used by Crosby, Minnesota. Credit: Walt Schryver.

Both Winther Motor Truck Company and Peter Pirsch and Sons were located in Kenosha, Wisconsin. Pirsch used a 1920 Winther chassis to build this triple combination. This picture is from an early advertisement.

Chapter 3
1921-1930

Some nationwide registration figures were found for late 1921. At that time there were 1.3 million trucks in the United States. Of these, 51 percent were Fords. The other makes, in descending order of popularity, were Republic, Reo, Dodge Brothers, White, International, Chevrolet, GMC, Autocar, Maxwell, and Overland. These 10 makes totaled 23 percent of the trucks.[1]

Harvey Firestone, of the tire company, was responsible for a post-World War I campaign to increase use of trucks. He developed the slogan "Ship by Truck," and cities were encouraged to have "Ship by Truck" parades. This would show their confidence in the use of trucks. Firestone also established 67 offices throughout the country to increase public awareness of trucks.[2]

While most drivers learned trucking on their own, there were also formal schools set up as early as 1920. Packard Motor Car Company, which built both trucks and cars then, ran one such program in St. Louis. It was known as the Packard Driver's Institute. The institute was also concerned with drivers' physical condition. As a result of physical examinations, several participants were fitted with eyeglasses. Much of the institute's program dealt with vehicle maintenance. According to the school's brochure, the following points were covered:

The Motor -- How gasoline is turned into power -- Practical study of assembled motor and parts

Carburetors -- Why they are used and what they do -- Practical demonstration of carburetor adjustment and care

Ignition -- How electricity is generated and stored for use in motor trucks

Water circulation system -- Cooling systems -- Thermostat -- Radiator -- Non-freezing solutions

Why oil is used and what it does -- Methods of application

Clutch and transmission -- Types -- Assembly -- Lubrication and care

The final drive -- Types of differentials -- Types of drive: worm, chain, internal gear, double reduction types

The truck chassis -- Brakes -- Steering gear -- Bearings[3]

Kenworth Trucks were introduced in 1923, and Coleman trucks in 1925. Truck and bus sales in 1929 totaled 881,000 units, the highest ever. Truck and bus registrations totaled about 3.6 million units. Because of the Depression, truck sales slumped. The 1929 figures would not be surpassed until 1941, when the nation geared up for another world war.

---

1. Harlan Appelquist, "American Truck Builders of 1939," **The Bulb Horn** (March/April 1974), page 30.
2. Alfred Lief, **Harvey Firestone** (New York, McGraw-Hill, 1951), page 188.
3. "Packard Driver's Institute, St. Louis," **Transportation Engineering Bulletins** (Detroit: Packard Motor Car Company, 1920), page 5.

At the end of the 1920s, a typical truck rode on pneumatic tires, had electric lights, an air cleaner, a windshield wiper, enclosed gears, and, probably all-wheel brakes (either mechanical or hydraulic). The cab was behind the engine. There was no streamlining except that the fenders were curved. Some trucks had shock absorbers, pressure lubrication, air brakes, oil filters, and mechanical turn indicators shaped like arms and controlled by cables from within the cab. The number of makes of trucks was probably less than 100. Many manufacturers sputtered and died during the Depression.

For fire apparatus in this decade, we see the largest number of different makes of commercial chassis employed. Rigs became larger, faster, and more dependable. By 1930, when most commercial trucks had an enclosed cab, fire apparatus still did not. Nor did they have side doors as it was believed fire fighters could respond more quickly if there were no doors to open. Booster pumps and tanks were becoming more common than chemical tanks. In 1921, Coalinga, California bought a Ford TT outfitted by Obenchain-Boyer with two chemical tanks and 500 feet of hose (the community relied on water pressure in its hydrant system). In 1929, a front-mount Darley pump was installed on this Ford TT.

This is probably the decade when all volunteer departments motorized. They had a large variety of chassis to purchase and to outfit. Many bought used trucks and placed chemical tanks on them. Toward the end of the decade, the W.S. Darley Company in Chicago began listing fire truck equipment in its municipal supplies catalog. This gave the "do-it-yourselfers" a supply of pumps, tanks, hose reels, etc., necessary to complete the job. There was such a wide variety of apparatus produced in this decade that this chapter of the book has the most pictures.

Communities and volunteers raised money for apparatus, using a number of methods. A few communities were fortunate enough to have the apparatus donated. For example, in 1924 a judge in Saybrook, Connecticut wrote to a prominent former resident "suggesting that inasmuch as he had always maintained a kindly feeling for the old town and visited it each summer, he might wish to donate fire apparatus to meet its needs."[4] The person responded positively and contributed $4000, which was used to purchase a American LaFrance/Brockway. At that point, a volunteer department was organized.

In 1925, *The American City* magazine surveyed several state fire fighters' associations to determine how they raised money. One question asked about fund-raising activities used, and answers included dances, minstrel shows, turkey raffles, oyster suppers, and sponsoring baseball games. Use of traveling carnivals was discussed, and one individual interviewed observed that "traveling carnivals are not much in demand in this state, as the rough element that travels with them has caused a feeling against that method of raising funds. The one-horse circus is also out of date, for these concerns, being mostly flim-flam artists, got more than the home fire company."[5] Also discussed were the issues of whether small communities should have a paid chief to lead the volunteers, and whether there were volunteer departments financed wholly by municipal funds so that they would not have to rely on volunteers' fund-raising efforts. At this time, many volunteer departments were quite independent of their municipal governments. The secretary of the Minnesota State Fire Department Association wrote:

"I am fully convinced that volunteer fire departments should be under the control of the municipal government and that the chief and assistant chief should be appointed by the council and paid a salary for their services. I would go even farther, and say that the village or town should set aside a certain sum of money each year for its fire protection. Out of this fund the volunteer firemen would be paid for whatever service they are called upon to render at fires; new equipment could be purchased from this fund, and replacements of old equipment could also be taken care of out of it. The time is not far distant when it will be almost necessary for the smaller towns or villages to adopt the budget system of running their municipal affairs, and the fire department should be figured in as it should be."[6]

Another device for covering costs was reported by the Albion, New York Volunteer Fire Department. They entered into contracts with surrounding communities to render service when needed. "A charge of $50 for a run within the three-mile limit is made and $3 for each additional mile or fraction, one way, is charged."[7] At that time (1927), the Albion fire department had 225 volunteers and three paid operators. A

4. *Undated materials supplied by the Old Saybrook Historical Society.*
5. **The American City** (May 1925), page 542.
6. *Ibid.*
7. **The American City** (July 1927), page 89.

number of communities with volunteer fire departments began paying volunteers small, regular amounts for responding to a fire call or for attending training. Many communities assumed responsibility for volunteers injured or killed in the line of duty.

In Saratoga, California, a fire district had been organized under state law in 1922, and the district had power to raise money by taxation. In 1924, the elected fire commissioners purchased a new Ford Model T combination chemical and hose car. (The fire station in Saratoga is housed in the building first built for the Interurban rail line. It once had a turntable to enable the street cars to change directions and served as a repair barn for the electric street cars. Later it functioned as a service station and then was converted to the firehouse.) In the early days of telephones in Saratoga, certain volunteers had an emergency fire response connection that would enable them to activate a loud air horn at the station to alert the volunteers. The first fireman to arrive at the station lifted the phone receiver and got the message as to the location and type of fire. In 1927, in nearby Los Gatos, the first pumping engine was place in service, a 750-gpm 1927 American LaFrance pumper. In the same year, a modern firehouse was erected.

In many communities, electric horns or sirens began taking the place of bells for summoning volunteers. In rural areas, the party-line telephone was used. Each farmer then drove to the fire, often bringing one or more milk cans filled with water. In Pocatello, Idaho, fire sirens were installed on buildings at major intersections and sounded to alert and clear traffic, allowing the fire apparatus to move through. Volunteers continued to assist the paid fire fighters. The shop whistle in the Oregon Short Line Railroad was used to summon volunteers. Switch engines in the rail yard were equipped with pumps and hoses to fight fires on the railroad's property.

When needed, all citizens will help. Here some are helping free an early '20s American LaFrance from the mud. Credit: General Tire.

Early fire trucks did not have windshields. W.S. Darley advertised driving goggles in one of its late '20s catalogs. Reinforced canvas windshields were also offered. One is shown on a 1922 Brockway LaFrance Torpedo used in Maine. The hole for a flood lamp is unusual. Brockway LaFrance Torpedos were a popular line of apparatus built by American LaFrance on Brockway chassis. Credit: Wayne Sorensen Collection.

This is a 1924 LaFrance Brockway Torpedo with two 40-gallon chemical tanks and hose body built for Bantam, Connecticut. Credit: Ed Hass.

Here's a 1926 Cosmopolitan Type 63 American LaFrance 400-gpm gear pump triple combination on a Brockway "Highway Express" chassis. Credit: American LaFrance.

A 1927 American LaFrance 400-gpm Cosmopolitan built on a Brockway "Highway Express" chassis for Central, New Mexico. Credit: Wayne Sorensen Collection.

This 1931 photo shows the Stanton, Iowa fire station and truck. The original caption said it was built by a man named Bergren who is standing on the left. A single chemical tank, hose reel, and ladder are visible. It's all carried on what looks like an early '20s Cadillac automobile chassis and body. Credit: State Historical Society of Iowa.

A 1928 Cadillac sedan was used to build a 500-gpm front mount triple combination for Worley, Idaho. The body work was done by Gray's Auto of Lewiston. Credit: Bill Hattersley.

A 1924 Chevrolet with hose body was used in Maine, New York. Credit: Don Wood.

The Erlton, New Jersey Volunteers used a 1926 Chevrolet chassis to mount an American LaFrance hose wagon body. Credit: Dick Adelman.

A 1927 Chevrolet chassis was used by Howe Fire Apparatus to build a small triple combination, with a 350-gpm rotary gear pump, for Albion, Pennsylvania. Credit: Howe Fire Apparatus.

Business end of a circa 1927 Chevrolet front-mount pumper. The suction hose is carried around the front of the rig. Credit: Chuck Rhodes.

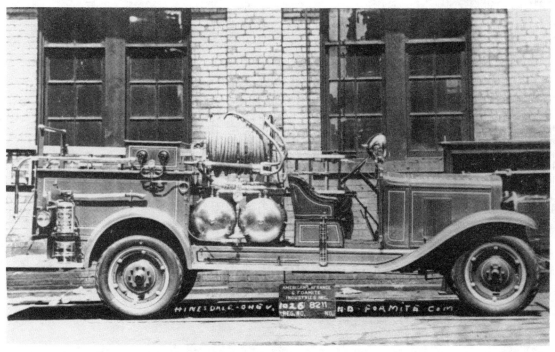

Hinsdale, Illinois used this 1930 Chevrolet with an American LaFrance chemical body. Credit: Wayne Sorensen Collection.

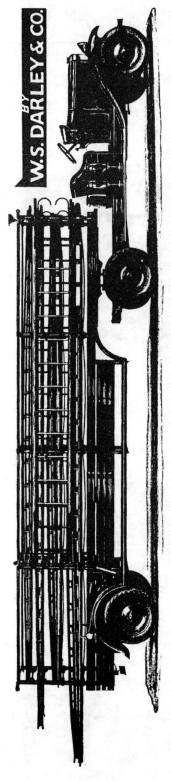

W.S. DARLEY & CO.

BY

BUILT FOR **FORD—CHEVROLET—REO** And Larger
MODEL AA TRUCKS

SPECIFICATIONS—SERIES A—SINGLE BANK TRUCK

Length of Ladder Chassis..20 feet
Width between Uprights...30½ inches
Running Board, 19 inches wide, length.............................7 feet
Front Fender Running Board, 19 inches wide, length...............32 inches
Front and Running Board Fenders are Rubber Covered.
Hose Box, capacity 500 feet......................16" deep by 16' 4½" long
Rear Tires, 6 ply....................................30" by 5"

Ladder   ⎰ Two Extension Ladders, length 45 feet.
Capacity   ⎱ Two Single Ladders, length 24 feet.
and   ⎰ Two Single Ladders on sides 24 feet.
Pike Poles ⎱ Pike Poles carried on top.

Hand Railings, Nickel Plated.
Fifth Wheel.....................................Spring Cushion Type
Rear Steering Wheel is extra equipment....Quick Detachable Steering Post
Locking Apparatus ⎰ Single Lever Locks all Ladders except the Side
                  ⎱ Ladders.

Powerful Searchlight and Big Chief Siren included.
Finished in bright fire department RED with GOLD LEAF trimming and
striping.
Approximate weight, without ladders.....................6000 lbs.
PRICE: Complete Ladder Chassis with Spring Cushion Fifth Wheel
adaptable to Ford, Chevrolet or Reo Motor Chassis. No ladders. See
our catalogs for ladder prices.
No. C555. Red Arrow Hook and Ladder Truck................**$995.00**

The finest truck equipment that money can buy.

The complete framework is electrically welded. No bolts to work loose—no body squeaks.

Running boards are wide and rubber covered. There is room for eight men on each side. A nickel plated hand rail is provided on each side and on the motor truck.

This truck will take over 200 feet of truss ladders or about 300 feet of solid side ladders. A single locking lever is provided to lock all the ladders, preventing them from shifting. Yet they can be released in an instant.

The hose box will carry 500 feet of hose.

City service semi-trailer pictured in a Darley catalog, circa 1930. The tractor is a Chevrolet. Catalog copy said, in part: "It is regularly furnished without a rear steering apparatus. We recommend this type to volunteer departments as it takes an experienced operator to steer a rear wheel steering apparatus and no one but an experienced man should be in charge." The price, without ladders, was $995, and the trailer could be adapted to a Ford, Chevrolet, or Reo tractor chassis. Credit: Darley.

A view inside the Fort Collins fire station, circa 1930. An alarm box is on the left wall. In the center is a 1930 Chevrolet city service truck which was assembled by the paid fire fighters in Fort Collins while they were on duty. The total out-of-pocket cost to the city was $4000. This rig was featured in ads by the W.S. Darley Company of Chicago, which sold (and to this day continues to sell) a wide range of municipal supplies through catalogs. Most of the equipment on this rig was supplied by Darley. Equipment on the truck included: a deck gun; nine ladders; plaster hooks; wire cutters; lanterns, soda and acid extinguishers; hose; gas masks; stretcher; blankets; life line; rope; safety belts; nozzles; claw hammers; nail sacks; 20 canvas salvage covers; two buckets; chain; rope and tackle; 18 door wedges; three squeegees; brooms; mops; shovels; pitchfork; foam generator; portable flood light; wrecking bars; pick ax; sledge hammer; first-aid kit; shingle remover; and various wrenches. Credit: Fort Collins Public Library.

East Grandy, Connecticut used this 1929 Chevrolet. The nameplate on the side of hood says "Suburban Fire Fighter," but we don't know who the outfitter was. The rig has a 350-gpm pump and a 200-gallon tank. Credit: Roland Boulet.

Commerce motor trucks were built in Detroit. Boyer Fire Apparatus Company of Logansport, Indiana used this Commerce chassis to build a chemical and hose car for Gifford, Indiana. Credit: Boyer Fire Apparatus Company.

Concord trucks were built by the Abbott-Downing Truck and Body Company of Concord, New Hampshire. This circa 1927 Concord chassis was used to build a 500-gpm triple combination for Bardwick, Vermont. Credit: Roland Boulet.

Corbitt trucks were built in Henderson, North Carolina. This one was equipped as a pumper. Credit: National Automotive History Collection, Detroit Public Library.

Day Elder Motor Truck Company of Irvington, New Jersey built the chassis for Fair Lawn, New Jersey's 350-gpm combination outfitted by Peter Pirsch and Sons of Kenosha, Wisconsin. The chemical tanks were removed and a 500-gpm skid pump installed behind the seat. Lettering on the side says, "Reserve Firemen Co. No. 1 C.D.V." Those words and the style of helmets hanging on the side indicate the rig was assigned to civil defense work at the time the picture was taken, probably during World War II. Credit: Dick Adelman.

DiMartini trucks were built in San Francisco during the 1920s. Mill Valley, California purchased this DiMartini with a chemical and hose body. Credit: Laurence F. Jonson.

Woodside, California built this 250-gpm pumper on a 1925 Dodge chassis. It carried a small water tank. Credit: John Graham.

Pocono Township Volunteer Fire Company of Tannersville, Pennsylvania, formed in 1940, purchased a used 1929 Dodge Brothers truck to build a 350-gpm front mount pump triple combination. Lettering on side says "Organized 1940." Credit: Ray Stevens.

Urbandale, Iowa used this mid-'20s Dodge that appears to be homemade. A single chemical tank can be seen behind driver. Over 12 buckets are nestled on the running board. They were probably needed to supply water for recharging the chemical tank. Credit: State Historical Society of Iowa.

The Dorris Motor Car Company of St. Louis, Missouri built the K-5 chassis for this rig used by Madison, Missouri. The pump has been removed. Credit: Chuck Rhodes.

The volunteers in Belmont, California converted a 1930 Fageol milk truck into this tanker. Credit: Wayne Sorensen Collection.

A 1926 Federal chassis used by Boyer to build this 500-gpm triple combination rig for Lakewood, Michigan, a volunteer department near Kalamazoo. Volunteers' helmets hang from side. Credit: Martin Sernatinger.

A 1924 Ford Model TT chassis used by Waterous Engine Works of St. Paul, Minnesota to build Christiana, Pennsylvania a combination chemical and hose cab. Credit: Waterous.

A 1925 Ford Model TT flatbed with water tank. Pump is mounted at the rear. Credit: Macomb County Historical Society, Mount Clemens, Michigan.

A 1923 Model T Ford chemical and hose wagon manned by volunteers for the Los Angeles, California Fire Department in the area now known as Canoga Park in the San Fernando Valley. Note siren on top of the garage to call volunteers. Credit: Dale Magee.

Jackson, Tennessee extended the frame of this 1924 Ford Model TT to build this ladder truck equipped with double chemical tanks. Notice lack of fenders over rear wheels. Hand-crank siren is on cowl. Credit: Wayne Sorensen Collection.

Edgewater, New York's Volunteer Hose #1 two-tank combination chemical hose was first used on the Rockefeller estate at Pocantico Hills, New Jersey. The body work for this 1924 Ford Model TT was by American LaFrance. Credit: Charles E. Beckwith.

This 1924 Ford triple combination has a 200-gpm pump, a small booster tank and large flood light. The body work and pump were installed by General Manufacturing Company, St. Louis, Missouri. This was Engine No. 1 for Lenzburg, Illinois. Credit: Dick Adelman.

An early airport crash/rescue rig was built on a Ford AA chassis by the Prospect Fire Engine Company of Prospect, Ohio. Note the dual front tires. A midship's pump has its gauges at the rear of the cab top. The vehicle had a boom crane and could also transport injured people. Credit: George Hanley.

A well-equipped city service body on a mid-'20s FWD chassis. Credit: FWD.

A 1930 FWD recovery vehicle was built for use in the Detroit-Windsor tunnel. It carries two chemical tanks, hose, and fire extinguishers. Credit: Motor Vehicle Manufacturers Association.

Beatrice, Nebraska's 1925 GMC K-101 triple combination with both a small pump and chemical tanks. Credit: Columbia Body & Equipment Company.

Farmington, Delaware purchased a 1927 GMC hose wagon from O.J. Childs Company of Utica, New York. Later it was converted to a tanker. Credit: John G. Robrecht.

An American LaFrance Pioneer Model with a 250-gpm front mount pump built on a 1928 GMC chassis with four-cylinder engine. Credit: American LaFrance.

American LaFrance built this 500-gpm, 1930 GMC pumper for Boulder Creek, California. The original pump was later replaced with a skid pump. Credit: Wayne Sorensen.

American LaFrance used a 1925 Graham Brothers "G-Boy" chassis to build a Type 4, four-35-gallon chemical tank car for Leesburg, New Jersey. Note hose coiled on top. Credit: American LaFrance.

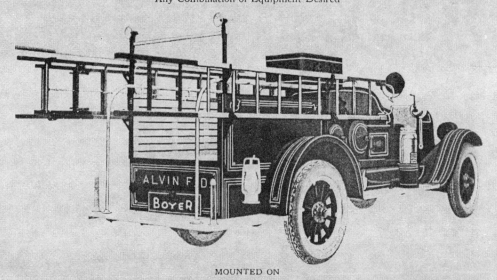

Apparatus outfitters sought to develop a reputation for outfitting various popular makes of commercial chassis. This Boyer ad, from the 1920s, says that its equipment can be used on Graham Brothers trucks. Close-up at top shows a chemical tank. Handle on top releases acid into the soda mixture in the tank. Crank at left is an agitator.

A 1926 Graham Brothers used in Woodland, California. Close-ups show rear view with tank, ladder, and hose reels; and chain drive linking driveshaft to pump mounted between driver's seat and tank. Rig was built by volunteers. Credit: Don Wood.

There was a close relationship between Dodge autos and Graham Brothers trucks. This is a 1929 Graham Brothers chassis used by American LaFrance to build a combination chemical and hose car for the Maribel Community Fire Department. Credit: American LaFrance.

Gotfredson Truck Corporation of Walkerville, Ontario built the 1928 chassis used by the Bickle Fire Engines Ltd. of Woodstock, Ontario, to build this triple combination for Kingsville, Ontario. Credit: Dick Adelman.

Grass-Premier trucks were built in Sauk City, Wisconsin. This one, from the late '20s, has a front-mount Champion pump, and was used by the Bear Creek Fire Department. Credit: Don Wood.

Remnants of a 1923 Hudson, once operated by the Nye County, Nevada fire department. A chemical tank and hose basket are visible. Credit: Bill West.

A 1922 International pumper demonstrates its ability to pump water to the top of a tall structure in Swansea, Massachusetts. Credit: Navistar Archives.

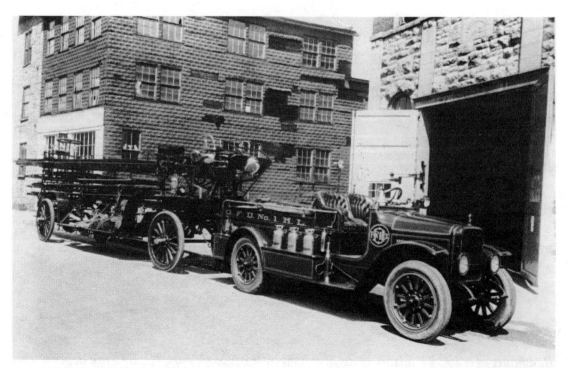

A 1923 International pulls a one-time horse-drawn aerial ladder rig with a tiller at the distant end. Credit: Navistar Archives.

This 1925 photo was taken in Dawson in the Yukon Territories, Canada. At left is an International with chemical tanks and overhead ladder racks. At right is a steam pump pulled by a crawler tractor. Credit: Public Archives of Canada.

A 1924 Kearns-Dughie chassis was used by the Foamite-Childs Corporation of Utica, New York to build a 750 triple combination for Morestown, New Jersey. Credit: Bill Schwartz.

The Foamite-Childs Corporation of Utica used an assembled Kearns-Dughie van chassis to build this 1927 600-gpm triple combination for Old Bridge, New Jersey. Notice the large round water tank. Credit: Charles E. Beckwith.

A 1927 Larrabee chassis was used by Buffalo Fire Appliance Corporation of Buffalo, New York to build this 500-gpm triple combination for Grantley, Pennsylvania. Credit: Wayne Sorensen Collection.

Larrabee-Deyo Motor Truck Company of Binghamton, New York provided the 1927 chassis for Spark Hill, New York's hose wagon. Credit: Wayne Sorensen Collection.

Neptune Township, New Jersey's squad car is mounted on a circa 1925 Lincoln commercial car chassis. Credit: Dick Adelman.

The Lincoln Motor Car Company built the 1929 commercial chassis for this sedan front-mount pumper used in Salem, West Virginia. Credit: Wayne Sorensen Collection.

Built by Adam Black Body Company of Jersey City on a Maccar chassis, this hose wagon was delivered in 1929 to E.H. Stokes Fire Company of Ocean Grove, New Jersey. The hose wagon was equipped with a "deck gun." Credit: William N. Schwartz.

While not a volunteer rig, this picture of a Mack tractor, circa 1920, illustrates two technological problems. The first was the development of a fifth wheel connecting the tractor to the trailer. Fire apparatus represented some of the earliest tractor-trailer combinations used, mainly because tractors were developed to take the place of horses. The second technological problem was finding power to raise the aerial ladder. In this picture we see a large compressed air tank; subsequent developments relied on the truck's own drivetrain. This rig was used by the fire department in Allentown, Pennsylvania, Mack's longtime hometown. Credit: Mack Museum.

A 1926 Mack AB Series combination chemical and hose car built for Long Branch, New Jersey. Volunteers' hats hang on the side. Credit: Rick Adelman.

A 1927 Mack, Type 15, Model-AP combination pump and hose car built for Lynbrook, New York. Helmets for nine volunteers hang above ladder. Credit: Gus Johnson.

This 1930 B series Mack 250-gpm combination was first in service in Pasadena, California, then in service at Bonny Doon, California. The B series was widely used in fire apparatus. Credit: Wayne Sorensen.

Stylish Marmon automobiles were built in Indianapolis. The company also built a few truck, bus, and commercial chassis. Waramosa, New Jersey's 1929 eight-cylinder Marmon combination hose and pump car had a front-mounted pump. Credit: Bill Schwartz.

This is Lindenhurst, New York's 1925 Maxwell combination chemical and hose car. Credit: Wayne Sorensen Collection.

Drafting from a stream with front-mounted pump on one of the California Division of Forestry's Morelands, circa 1930. Morelands were built in Southern California. Credit: Forestry Library, University of California-Berkeley.

Nash was a well-known auto builder and, for a short time, produced trucks. American LaFrance built this Type 2 combination chemical and hose on a 1922 Nash chassis for Battle Creek, Michigan. Credit: American LaFrance.

Here's Gilman, Wisconsin's 1926 Nott-Universal pumper powered by a Continental engine. It had a 500-gpm Northern pump. Between two headlights a narrow pipe is visible, leading to the top of the radiator. When pumping water, some water could be diverted through this pipe to help cool the engine. Credit: Walt Schryver.

A 1928 Nott-Universal 500-gpm triple combination built for Brownton, Minnesota. Credit: Dick Adelman.

A 1921 Packard outfitted by Pirsch with a pump and chemical tank. Photo taken at an auction in Sparta, Wisconsin in 1988. Credit: Don Wood.

The two photos are of the same rig, a 1923 Oshkosh with all-wheel-drive outfitted by Pirsch, for use in Black River Falls, Wisconsin. It had both chemical tanks and a 500-gpm pump. Side view is a factory shot, taken when the rig was new. Front quarter photo was taken in 1974. Credit: Pirsch, and Walt Schryver.

Paramount automobiles were made in Hagerstown, Maryland in the late 1920s. This one was used as a small tanker/brush rig in Throggs Neck, New York. Backpack pump is just behind the seat. Lettering on the side says, "Edgewater Vol. Hose Company No. 1, Inc." Credit: Charles Beckwith.

A 1926 Pierce-Arrow Z-chassis with a chemical and pumper body by Boyer was used by Larchmont Grosse Point Park, Michigan. Credit: Smithsonian Institution.

Two views of a 1922 Reo combination chemical and hose wagon, owned and operated by the Parchment Paper Mill and manned by volunteers in Parchment, Michigan. It was taken out of service in 1952. Credit: Martin Sernatinger.

A 1923 Reo combination and hose car is shown in an early advertisement for Childs fire equipment. Text of the ad says: "For Any Type of Chassis." Credit: Wayne Sorensen Collection.

A 1925 Reo Speedwagon Model B chassis was used by American LaFrance to build this Type 4 four-tank chemical car for South Vineland, New Jersey. Credit: American LaFrance.

The Sims Fire Equipment Company of San Antonio, Texas used a 1925 Reo chassis and a 500-gpm Hale pump to build this triple combination for Hondo, Texas. Credit: Dick Adelman.

W.S. Nott Company of Minneapolis utilized a 1929 Reo Speedwagon chassis to build a 500-gpm pumper for Osakis, Minnesota. Credit: Dan G. Martin.

The Sanford Motor Truck Company of Syracuse, New York built this impressive-looking 600-gpm rotary gear pumper for Towaco, New Jersey. This 1929 truck has whitewall tires and an aluminum radiator shell. Credit: Richard Adelman.

Clayton, New York converted this 1928 Sanford 500-gpm triple combination into a 35-foot aerial ladder truck. The ladder is of a type used by utilities and tree trimmers. Credit: William Adams.

A 1923 Sanford Greyhound "Speed Truck" chassis was used for this 500-gpm pumper built by Obenchain-Boyer for Port Byron, New York. Credit: Dan G. Martin.

Sanford trucks and fire apparatus were built in Syracuse. This 1927 model, with a 500-gpm pump and a Continental engine, went to a community fire company in New Jersey. It's shown parked in front of a dealer for Goodrich fire hose. Credit: Sanford.

Ahrens-Fox introduced its Schacht chassis 500-gpm Model V rotary pumper in 1930. This one was registered No. 7004 and went to White House, New Jersey. Credit: Bill Schwartz.

Schacht trucks were built in Cincinnati starting in 1910. Here's a 1930 Schacht chassis outfitted by Ahrens-Fox, also of Cincinnati, for Menlo Park, California. Rig has a 500-gpm pump. Credit: Ahrens-Fox.

This is a 1925 Selden combination chemical and hose car manufactured by Selden Bros. of Flowerton, Pennsylvania for use in Fort Washington, Pennsylvania. Credit: Dick Adelman.

This is Port Monmouth, New Jersey's 1926 Buffalo pumper built on a Selden chassis. Credit: Bill Schwartz.

A 1925 Star Compound Six chassis was used to build a hose car for Rockaway, New Jersey. Credit: Frank Fenning Jr.

A three-tank chemical car was built on a 1924 Stewart chassis by Buffalo Fire Apparatus for East Greenbush, New York. Credit: Buffalo Fire Apparatus Corp.

Stoughton trucks were built by the Stoughton Wagon Company of Stoughton, Wisconsin. This Stoughton chassis from the mid-'20s was used to build a 350-gpm triple combination with two 40-gallon chemical tanks for Clarksville, Iowa. Credit: Wayne Sorensen Collection.

Boyd, Wisconsin's 350-gpm triple combination was built on 1927 Stoughton chassis. Credit: Walt Schryver.

A 1928 Studebaker chassis was used by Pirsch to build a 500-gpm pumper for the Richfield, Wisconsin Volunteer Fire Company. Credit: Dick Adelman.

The Transport Truck Company was located in Mount Pleasant, Michigan. Huntington Woods, Michigan's combination chemical and hose car was built on a 1921 Transport chassis. Later, a 500-gpm pump replaced the chemical tank. Credit: Wayne Sorensen Collection.

Here's a 1921 White 500-gpm triple combination with chemical tank, built for the Eagle Hose Company of Dickson City, Pennsylvania. It has a Hale pump. Credit: John Sytsma.

Two city service trucks with chemical tanks on a 198-inch wheelbase 1926 White chassis. The upper one went to Perry, New York, and the lower one to Bar Harbor, Maine. Credit: Volvo/White.

Personnel working in industrial plants functioned as a form of volunteers as they were expected to man the plant's own apparatus in case of a fire. This photo, which originally ran in a 1929 issue of a White Motor Company house organ, shows a White with chemical tanks, owned by Shell Oil Company, fighting a gas fire in Santa Fe Spring, California. The Shell emblem is on the side of the seat and on the front of the top tank. The fire was extinguished by tunneling 50 feet below the surface of the earth to divide the gas into several smaller channels that could be extinguished individually. Credit: Volvo/White.

A 1930 Willys-Overland chassis was used by W.S. Nott Fire Engine Company to build this 500-gpm "Victor" model pumper for Bowler, Wisconsin. Credit: Walt Schryver.

Pirsch used a Winton motor car commercial chassis to build a chemical and hose car for Grand Haven, Michigan. Credit: Pirsch.

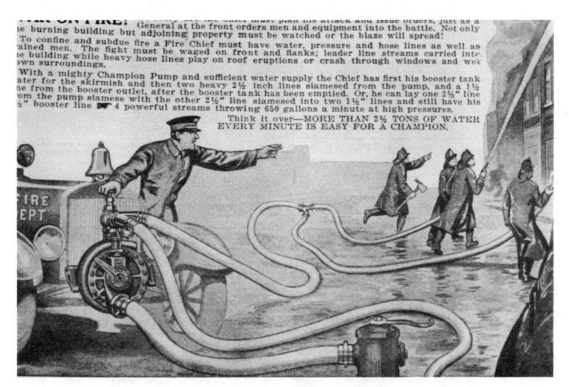

Pictures of front-mounted pumps are advertised in 1930 W.S. Darley catalogs. Credit: W.S. Darley.

Chapter 4
1931-1940

1931-1940 was also an important decade with respect to the development of trucks and truck equipment. As early as 1932, diesel engines were offered with Indiana, Sterling, and Kenworth trucks. Ford's first V-8s were available for trucks at about the same time. By the end of the '30s, other trucks had six-cylinder engines and hydraulic brakes on all wheels. Hydraulic valve lifters and synchromesh transmissions were common.

However, truck production in 1932 dropped to about one-quarter of 1929's level because of the Depression. This was hard on both manufacturers and dealers. Fire apparatus historian Walt McCall wrote: "Orders for new fire equipment had shrivelled to a mere trickle. In some plants there was barely enough work to keep the place open. The work force and the sales staff had been cut to the bone."[1]

Many communities were stretched for dollars when it came to paying for new apparatus. This shortage of cash and abundance of labor resulted in a large crop of "homemade" rigs using relatively inexpensive truck chassis. We would also guess that sales of rigs on commercial chassis probably increased as a percent of total apparatus sales since they were more affordable. A W.S. Darley ad aimed at Chevrolet dealers said:

" If your town, or any village, town or community in your territory is considering the purchase of new fire apparatus, you will have first consideration if you tell them about [Darley's] Champion Fire Apparatus which is priced 25 to 40% less than other apparatus. UNDER OUR PLAN YOU FURNISH THE CHASSIS -- it's your deal. We build the rest of the equipment.... Under our plan you have the factory deliver the chassis to us in Chicago.... We do the rest, and when it's ready you can come and drive it away on hard roads that lead in all directions.... Champion Chevrolet Fire Apparatus is a good advertisement for your trucks...." [2]

In the same catalog was a testimonial from the fire chief of Eastport, New York saying that his department's Darley "Champion fire pump lifted water eight feet from a lake and pushed it through fourteen hundred feet of two and one-half inch hose up a five percent grade from one o'clock in the afternoon until five o'clock the next morning in order to flood the basement of the schoolhouse in which about two hundred tons of coal were on fire."

Volunteer departments that could afford to began retiring their Ford Ts and TTs and replacing them with newer apparatus on Ford V-8, Chevrolet, Dodge, International, and Reo chassis. Davis, California purchased a 1931 Chevrolet with a 400-gpm pump. Bundles of 200 feet of 2-1/2-inch hose were at the rear and could be dropped from the driver's seat at the site of a fire.

---

*1. Walter P. McCall, **American Fire Engines Since 1900** (Glen Ellyn, IL: Crestline, 1976), page 139.*
*2. 1938 Chevrolet **Silver Book**, page 58.*

In 1934, Coalinga, California purchased a Dodge for $657 and a 350-gpm Barton pump which was installed by Van Pelt in Oakdale, California. In 1936, Coalinga purchased a Ford chassis for $787, and a Barton 600-gpm pump for $895, and also had it installed by Van Pelt. The truck with pump was then returned to a local body shop in Coalinga where the hose body was built and a booster tank installed, along with other equipment, including a 47-foot extension ladder on a roof rack. The first pumping engine in Saratoga, California was a 1938 Diamond T 500-gpm pumper purchased from Food Machinery Company. Nearby, in Campbell, the volunteers were receiving nationwide publicity since so many of them responded on bicycles, but the memory of the "Pedal and Pump" fire department did not last. In 1937, the first motorized pumping engine was purchased from Van Pelt Fire Apparatus Company of Oakdale, California. This 500-gpm triple combination was mounted on an Indiana truck chassis. In 1939, a second 500-gpm triple combination was also purchased from Van Pelt and mounted on an Indiana chassis. Pocatello, Idaho replaced its 20-year-old Cadillac chemical rig with a racy Graham Paige roadster carrying a small booster tank and pump in the trunk and a fire extinguisher on the running board. It was also used as a resuscitator car.

In Iola, Wisconsin, volunteers performed fire inspections, with one report reading: "Carl Mortenson Pool Hall -- One of the heating stoves has a bad hole in the fire pot. Not safe to use."

Literature for the S.S. Albright Company, a Sacramento body builder, showed their apparatus bodies on Dodge, Ford, and International chassis. Their literature stressed that apparatus "must be sturdy to the highest degree. The weight of the entire equipment must be kept down as low as possible. Center of gravity must be kept low for safety and mobility." These weights were given for a rig with a 400-gallon tank on a two- or three-ton truck chassis: equipment, 2900 pounds; water, 3300 pounds; and chassis, 4800 pounds, for a total of 11,000 pounds.

The appearance of trucks changed during the 1930s. Many borrowed styling from automobiles. We think of car streamlining as beginning in the early 1930s. By the mid-1930s, streamlining had reached trucks. They had chrome grilles, separate parking lights on top of their fenders, two-piece V-windshields, tilted back. By late in the '30s, cab-over-engine models were offered by most manufacturers, although few were used in the fire service. Enclosed cabs were being used for apparatus, especially for that on commercial chassis. Some apparatus was completely enclosed.

The number of makes of trucks had declined. Many of those makes in 1939 are makes we have today, or at least can recall. Harlan Appelquist, an automotive historian, determined there were 30 makes of full-size trucks built in the United States in 1939.[3] They were: Autocar; Available; Biederman; Brockway; Brown; Chevrolet; Corbitt; Diamond T; Dodge; Duplex; Federal; Ford; Freightliner (which were built in the Pacific Northwest starting in 1939, and initially the firm was owned by and built rigs for Consolidated Freightways, a large motor carrier); F.W.D.; GMC; Gramm; Hendrickson; Hug; Indiana; International; Kenworth; Mack; Marmon-Herrington; Moreland; Nelson-LeMoon; Oshkosh; Peterbilt (whose production began in 1939, using facilities once used for building the Fageol truck); Reo; Schacht; Sterling; Stewart; Studebaker; Walter; and White.

This was the decade when the truck reached a high level of development. One could generalize that both trucks and fire apparatus of 1940 were comparable, in many respects, to those of today. The changes and improvements since 1940 are smaller in number and in degree than those prior to that date. Fire apparatus of 1940 had a modern, rugged look and performed well.

By the end of this decade, the nation's interest was focused on wars that were occurring in both Europe and Asia. Bombs dropped in cities created fires, destruction, and death on a scale that existing fire departments were unable to conquer.

---

3. Harlan Appelquist, "American Truck Builders of 1939," *The Bulb Horn* (March/April 1974), pages 30-34.

In the early 1930s, large automobile coupes could be outfitted with a fifth wheel for pulling semi-trailers. This 1931 Buick auto pulls a tillered ladder semitrailer. Originally, the trailer had been horse-drawn. It was used in Walnut Creek, California. Credit: Paul Darrell.

This 1938 photo, taken at a fire site in South Carolina's Sumter National Forest, shows a 1934-'35 Chevrolet 1-1/2-ton stake truck discharging fire fighters. An implement compartment is at the front of the truck bed, and the fire fighter at the far left is being outfitted with an Indian back pack pump that could carry five gallons of water. License plates show the truck was operated by the Civilian Conservation Corps, a federal agency that employed young men during the Depression. Credit: Forest Service, U.S.D.A.

A 1935 Chevrolet with front-mounted pump and water tank served the Pennsuaken Fire Company No. 6 of Highland, Pennsylvania. The bumper is split to protect the pump. Credit: John G. Robrecht.

A 1937 Chevrolet with pump mounted under the seat. The Burnett, Texas Fire Department had this built by Seagrave. Credit: Seagrave/FWD.

Howard-Cooper of Seattle, Washington used a 1937 Chevrolet chassis to build a triple-combination 500-gpm pumper for Nome, Alaska. It is equipped with a Seagrave all-bronze centrifugal pump and a water tank. Credit: Howard-Cooper.

A 1937 Chevrolet with a hose wagon body was used in South Floral Park, Long Island, New York. Note the double horn on the roof of the station to summon volunteers. Credit: Charles E. Beckwith.

A 1938 Chevrolet with pumper body installed by General of Detroit. Credit: National Automotive History Collection, Detroit Public Library.

Cranston Heights, Delaware bought this 1940 Chevrolet. U.S. Fire Apparatus built the hose body and installed the pump and water tank. Credit: Ray Stevens.

This 1940 Chevrolet COE was used in Amherst, Wisconsin. The photo taken at the Iola Fire Muster in 1992. Credit: Krause Publications.

General of Detroit used a 1937 Diamond T chassis to build a 500-gpm triple-combination for Brookview, New Jersey. Credit: Jim Burner.

Arbor Hose Co. No. 1 of Piscataway, New Jersey purchased this 500-gpm Quad from Peter Pirsch and Sons. The rig was mounted on a 1937 Diamond T chassis. Credit: Dick Adelman.

A 1937 Diamond T 301 chassis by Peter Pirsch and Sons was used to build a 500-gpm pumper for Stone Harbor, New Jersey. Nameplate on the side of the hood says: "SMOKEATER." Credit: Peter Pirsch and Sons.

Buffalo Fire Appliance Corporation of Buffalo, New York used a 1939 Diamond T chassis to build this attractive 500-gpm sedan pumper for the volunteer fire company in Hatfield, Pennsylvania. Credit: Jim Burner.

Looking like an expensive limousine from the front, this 1940 Diamond T was outfitted with a pumper body by Ward LaFrance. Credit: Hammond Adams.

A 1933 Dodge Brothers chassis was used to build Cranbury, New Jersey's 500-gpm combination. Credit: Bill Schwartz.

A 1933 Dodge Brothers chassis with a 350-gpm Barton front mount is now used as a muster rig by Cambria, California. Credit: Wayne Sorensen.

American LaFrance Type 36 built on a 1935 Dodge chassis with a 500-gpm rotary gear pump was built for Marlboro, New York. Credit: American LaFrance.

Chrysler Airstream and DeSoto Airflow models are well known. During the same period, some Dodge Airflow trucks were also built. This 1936 model was used in Teaneck, New Jersey. It was equipped for many duties, including brush fires; note backpack pumps, broom, and early crew cab. Credit: Dick Adelman.

San Carlos, California's 1938 Dodge 250-gpm Engine 1. Credit: John Graham.

Ward LaFrance of Elmira Heights, New York built a 500-gpm pumper on a 1939 Dodge chassis for Oswego, New York. Rear fenders have skirts. Credit: Dick Adelman.

Challenger Fire Equipment Company of Sacramento, California used a 1931 Fageol chassis to build Winters, California's tank wagon with a 35-gpm Viking pump and 500-gallon water tank. Sealed beam headlights later replaced the original lights. Three backpack pumps are on the running boards, indicating the rig fought some brush and grass fires. Credit: Wayne Sorensen Collection.

A 1931 Ford Model AA chassis was used by Maxim Motor Company to build a hose wagon for Marshfield, Massachusetts. Credit: Maxim Motor Company.

Andover, New Jersey is the owner of this 350-gpm pumper built on a 1931 Model A Ford chassis. The dual rear wheels made for better control of the vehicle and allowed it to carry more weight. The turn out gear was carried on the side of rig. Credit: Jim Burner.

This 1931 Ford Booster Wagon was built by American LaFrance for Perry, New York. Notice the single tires on the rear wheels and two booster reels. Credit: American LaFrance.

Fighting forest fires could take many days. Trucks used for fighting these fires had to carry and supply many fire fighters. The original caption on this photo said that it carried equipment for 50 men. It's a Ford Model AA used in New Hampshire's White Mountain National Forest. Coils of hose are carried both inside the box and hanging on the side. The truck is carrying a generator and reels of wire. Credit: Forest Service, U.S.D.A.

The Sugar Grove Community Fire Company used this pumper on a 1932 Ford Model AA chassis built by Seagrave. On the running board are six nested metal buckets. Credit: Seagrave/FWD.

An early Ford V-8 was the "B" model introduced in 1933. This one, with a Howe pump, is shown pumping water. Firemen everywhere liked the V-8's snappy performance.

VALUE BEYOND BELIEF $964

f. o. b. Chicago
and
Detroit

No. F1 Ford Chassis
Fire Dept Truck

The price of this Champion Fire Truck, $964.00 includes the Ford Chassis and seat and cowl, Champion Front Drive Fire Pump and Valves, Steel Hose Body, Steel Booster Tank and Connections, Booster Hose Basket, Steel Platform Step, Brass Railings, Brass Hold-on Bar, Flood Lights, Fresnel Red Lights, Electric Lantern Brackets, Suction Hose Channel, Ladder Locks, Steel Tool Box and F. D. Name Plates.

☛ Read the Specifications Next Column!

Other Equipment! Such as Fire Hose, Suction Hose, Nozzles, Playpipes, Siren, Hand Extinguishers, Bell, Fire Axes, Ladders, Etc., are sold separately—at very low prices—because Fire Chiefs must have a choice of such items, according to their requirements or local conditions. We have the largest and most complete line of fire department equipment in the WORLD, a few items of which are illustrated in this catalog.

Rear View of Champion Fire Engine showing how compactly the ladder equipment is carried. Also note the wide steel Platform Step and the equipment it carries. Also notice the Booster Tank and Hose Basket set forward and the rear loading space for fire hose in the body.

SPECIFICATIONS—PLEASE READ CAREFULLY

Ford, 4 Cylinder, New 1932 Model B Commercial Truck. and open Cab with seat. Extra heavy rear Spring with 13 leaves, and Six-Ply rear Tires.

Body—Standard All Steel Pick-Up Body by Ford Motor Co, to fit the chassis, ample load space, with 16-inch sides. Capacity, 500 feet, 2½ single jacket fire hose. ☛ The above, complete, will be furnished and serviced by your own ☛ local authorized Ford Dealer; f. o. b. Detroit, for...... **$410.00**

Steel Platform Step for Body. Made of Diamond Pattern Pressed Steel, flanged and drilled, ready for mounting. Aluminum coated.

Front, Side, Cross Bar and Step Railings. Solid Polished Brass with malleable flanges and fittings for extra strength.

Steel Booster Hose Basket. Made of Rolled Steel with Perforated Metal ends. Reinforced with 3 cross bars. Angle iron support bars attached. Capacity 150 feet of 1½-inch Booster Tank Fire Hose.

Champion Fire Pump. Complete with all attachment Brackets, Main Valve, Booster Valve, 3-inch Suction Inlet, Booster Connections, Automatic Primer, Tank Shut-off, Tank Connections, Gauge, Oil Cups, Etc. For Direct Connected Front Drive.

Booster Tank. 60 gallon capacity. Built of rustless ARMCO steel. All electrically hand welded. Made with deep easy filling trough. Flanged opening in bottom. Attachment brackets welded in place. Fire department RED.

Ladder Locks on both sides to hold Extension Ladder and Wall Ladder. Integral with the side railings.

Flood Lights. Two Dietz Fire Dept Flood Lights for Hold-on bar, Chromium plated with universal swivel brackets.

Red Fresnel Lights. Two, Fire Dept Type, for mounting on Hose basket. Chromium plated.

Electric Lantern Brackets. Two, aluminum, for holding Firemen's Delta lanterns.

Suction Hose Channel. Steel with running board brackets for carrying two lengths of suction hose.

Steel Tool Box carried on running board.

Fire Dept Name Plates. Polished aluminum insignia F. D. plates, for ornamentation and trim.

Bolts, Etc. All step bolts, cap screws, nuts, lock washers, etc., to completely put the job together.

Paint, Etc. 1 gallon of our special Fire Dept Red for painting chassis body and parts. Sufficient glass stain to color head light lens red and green.

All the above, from W. S. Darley & Co, f.o.b. Chicago... Assembly by local Ford dealer.....................$36.00 **$518.00**

Chassis, Pump and Body Equipment, Total............. **$964.00**

☛ DEDUCTIBLE, $15.54! This amount can be saved by customers who take advantage of the 3% Discount allowed by W. S. Darley & Co when cash is sent with order. Sending us cash with order ($502.46) reduces the total to $948.46.

5

Full-page ad in Darley's 1933 catalog advertises a completely equipped rig for $964, mounted on a Ford model B chassis with a four-cylinder engine. The new V-8 cost $50 more. Credit: W.S. Darley.

A 1934 Ford V-8 open-seat city service truck was used by Limestone, Maine. Sealed beam headlights were installed later. Credit: Dan Martin.

This is a 1934 Ford BB chassis with a 50-foot Pirsch electric aerial. The heavy locomotive bell on the front of the rig is used to counterbalance the aerial ladder. This rig is owned by Lake City, Minnesota. Note outrider jack on side. Credit: Ray Sharyer.

The Seagrave Corporation of Columbus, Ohio used a 1935 Ford V-8 chassis to build a triple combination with 500-gpm centrifugal pump for Gloucester City, New Jersey. Credit: John G. Robrecht.

A 1935 Ford/Buffalo with a 350-gpm pump was used in Reinerton, Pennsylvania. It was still in service in 1982 and is shown carrying four oxygen tanks for recharging masks. Credit: Roland Boulet.

Chatham, New Jersey's 1935 Ford V-8 city service truck. Credit: Dick Adelman.

Pacific Fire Extinguisher Company of Los Angeles, California built this 1935 Ford 500-gpm pumper for the Ashland Fire District near Oakland, California. It was rebuilt in 1948 by Coast. Credit: Paul Darrell.

This 500-gpm triple combination, for Newville, Pennsylvania, was built on a 1936 Ford chassis by the Ward LaFrance Truck Corporation, which usually built custom fire apparatus on their own chassis. Credit: Dick Adelman.

A 1936 Ford V-8 chassis was used by Eaton Metal Products to build a 250-gpm front mount pumper for Gold Hill, Colorado. Credit: Dick Adelman.

A 1936 Ford triple combination with gun and 500-gpm front-mounted pump was in service at West Memphis, Arkansas. Note racks in front for hose. Credit: Dick Adelman.

A 1937 Ford pumper outfitted with Seagrave equipment was used by the Parma Heights, Ohio Volunteer Fire Department. Credit: Seagrave/FWD.

A Seagrave-outfitted 1937 Ford was destined for a volunteer fire department. Credit: Seagrave/FWD.

A 1937 Ford V-8 chassis with chrome radiator shell was used by W.S. Darley & Company of Chicago to build this 500-gpm triple combination for Totowa, New Jersey. Credit: Dick Adelman.

This 1938 Ford/Howe was operated by Sellersville, Pennsylvania. The original pump has been replaced by an independently powered skid pump. Credit: Dick Adelman.

Middleton, Idaho volunteers built this 250-gpm front-mount pump triple combination on a 1938 Ford chassis. The pump is a Barton. Credit: Wayne Sorensen Collection.

FWD Corporation of Clintonville, Wisconsin built this 1931 500-gpm pumper for West Bend, Wisconsin. It was one of the first engines with an enclosed cab. Credit: FWD.

FWD Corporation furnished the chassis for this 1936 Pirsch 750-gpm pumper for Ishpeming, Michigan. Credit: FWD.

Oconto Falls, Wisconsin used this late '30s FWD pumper. Credit: FWD.

A 1937 GMC was used by Fair Lawn, New Jersey to build a front-mount pumper, rated at 500-gpm. Metal mesh replaced the original grille. Credit: Dick Adelman.

The General Fire Truck Corporation of St. Louis called their assembled unit the General Monarch. This 1933 model was used in Ligonier, Indiana. It had a 600-gpm pump, and pump controls were mounted in the cowl. Pictures were taken at an auction in Sparta, Wisconsin in 1988. Credit: Don Wood.

A 1938 GMC COE (cab over engine) chassis was used by General of Detroit to build this 750-gpm quad for Coldwater, Michigan. Credit: General Fire Truck Corporation, Detroit, Michigan.

City service body on a 1940 GMC chassis. Credit: Motor Vehicle Manufacturers Association.

Leonardo, New Jersey purchased this 1936 Stutz built on an Indiana chassis with a Town & Country hose bed. (Instead of side walls on the rig, it was equipped with a V-shaped tank. The tank was built as one unit on both sides and at the front, and it carried 350 gallons of water.) The pump was of 500-gpm capacity, and the rig had a lattice bumper. Credit: Bill Schwartz.

New Stutz Fire Apparatus Company of Hartford City, Indiana was the successor of Stutz Fire Engine Company of Indianapolis. Arnold, Pennsylvania purchased this triple-combination built on a 1932 Indiana chassis. Credit: Lynn Sams.

A 1939 Indiana-Van Pelt 500-gpm triple-combination, used in Campbell, California. Headlights are not original. Credit: Wayne Sorensen.

Obion, Tennessee ran this 1935 International C-30 triple-combination with a 500-gpm Barton front mount pump. Credit: Dick Adelman.

Maywood Chemical Works built their own fire truck on a 1936 International C chassis. Helmets, coats and boots are carried on the side of the truck. Maywood, New Jersey is the location of the chemical works. Credit: Dick Adelman.

A 1940 D series International with 250-gpm pump with a 500-gallon water tank built by Van Pelt for the Salinas, California Rural Fire Department. Note the double front bumper. Credit: John Graham.

Upper Saddle River, New Jersey used a 1939 International D-400 chassis to mount an Office of Civil Defense 500-gpm skid pump and a hose box from an American LaFrance to build their Engine 2. Note backpack pumps. Credit: Dick Adelman.

Two views of a 1939 Kenworth with an enclosed cab used by the Spokane County Fire Department in Washington. It had a Hale pump. Credit: Paccar.

Two views of a 1940 Kenworth 750-gpm pumper bound for Snohomish, Washington. This rig was powered by a Hercules engine and was outfitted by Curtis-Heiser. Credit: Paccar.

Pirsch used a 1932 LeBlond Schacht chassis to build a 500-gpm combination for Matawan Township, New Jersey. Credit: John J. Robrecht.

Ahrens-Fox merged with the LeBlond-Schacht Truck Company in 1936. Smaller fire engines were built on the Schacht chassis. This 500-gpm triple combination Ahrens-Fox Model SR. The "S" indicates the chassis is Schacht and the "R" means equipped with rotary gear pump. Rig built in 1938 for Parma, Ohio. Credit: Ahrens-Fox.

Another form of "volunteer" fire departments were associated with large institutions, such as hospitals, colleges, or prisons. Their own apparatus was stationed on the grounds, and various employees were trained to operate it during emergencies. Lettering on the side of this well-equipped early '30s Mack pumper says: "Illinois Department of Public Welfare, Lincoln State School and Colony." Credit: George Humphrey.

Woodside, California purchased this 1933 Mack B Series 500-gpm short wheelbase pumper with a "squirrel tail" suction and a front-mounted siren. Later, the rig was sold to Salida, California. Credit: John Graham.

Awaiting restoration is this 1936 Mack Jr. pumper. Close-up shows a Luverne pump under the seat. Originally it served Jessup, Iowa, and, for a short - and sad - period, was used for delivering pizzas. Credit: Don Nelson.

A 1940 Oshkosh chassis, powered by a Hercules engine, was used by Howe to build a 500-gpm pumper with a 250-gallon tank for Black River Falls, Wisconsin. Co-author Don Wood's grandparents lived in that community, and Wood recalls admiring this particular truck from the time he had to look up to read the word "Oshkosh" on the nameplate at the top of the grille. Credit: Walt Schryver.

A 1938 Packard chassis used by General of Detroit to build a 750-gpm triple combination for the Granite City Steel Company Fire Department in Granite City, Illinois. Credit: Wayne Sorensen Collection.

A 1938 Packard chassis was used by General of Detroit to build a 750-gpm triple combination for Reisterton, Maryland. Credit: General Fire Truck Corporation.

A 1938 Packard V-12, by General of Detroit, was used by the Grand Ledge, Michigan Fire Department. Owners of Walt McCall's **American Fire Engines Since 1900** may compare this photo with one of the rig when it had aged. Credit: National Automotive History Collection, Detroit Public Library.

The Pompton Falls Volunteer Fire Department used this 1932 Reo. The windshield is folded down; and turnout gear hangs on both sides. Credit: National Automotive History Collection, Detroit Public Library.

A 1932 Reo Speedwagon chassis was used to build a 400-gpm triple combination with a Barton front-mounted pump for Windsor, Pennsylvania. Credit: Dick Adelman.

Seagrave installed this pumper body on a 1936 Reo. The user was the St. Mary's Volunteer Fire Department in West Virginia. Credit: Seagrave/FWD.

This Reo-Seagrave from the late 1930s was used by the Dublin, Ohio Volunteer Fire Department. The rig is a triple combination. Credit: Seagrave/FWD.

Iola, Wisconsin bought this 1937 Reo during World War II and had it converted to a fire engine. Note the overhead ladder racks. The photo was taken at the Iola Fire Muster in 1992. Credit: Krause Publications.

This is a 1931 Stewart chassis outfitted by Buffalo Fire Apparatus Corporation for Lenox, Massachusetts. Credit: Dan G. Martin.

Blawnox, Pennsylvania used this 1936 Stewart chassis, outfitted as a 500-gpm pumper by Buffalo. Credit: Dan G. Martin.

The Stewart Motor Corporation of Buffalo, New York built the 1938 chassis used by the Sanford Fire Apparatus Corporation of East Syracuse to build this 500-gpm triple combination. Women are in the front seat; unusual at this time. Credit: Bill Schwartz.

The Obenchain-Boyer Company of Logansport, Indiana used a 1933 Studebaker to build this front-mount pumper for Hose Co. No. 1, Bloomsberg, New Jersey. Credit: Bill Schwartz.

Although probably not a volunteer rig, this 1934 Studebaker with a city service body is an example of using a commercial chassis - probably a school bus chassis - for a longer rig. Credit: Dan G. Martin.

Ahrens-Fox built but a few pumpers on commercial chassis. This Ahrens-Fox 500-gpm centrifugal triple combination was built in 1939 on a Studebaker chassis for Arlington Heights, Ohio. Credit: Ahrens-Fox.

A 1940 Studebaker destined for use by Patterson Township. The pump is beneath the seat; part of the cab door has been cut away. Credit: Blackhawk Classic Auto Collection.

In military posts, both civilian and military fire-fighting personnel were used. USA fire-fighting rigs were built in U.S. Army Ordnance shops between the two world wars, utilizing leftover World War I truck chassis. In this photo, taken in 1943 at Fort Reno, Oklahoma, we see on the left a QMC (standing for Quartermaster Corps) Type 50 750-gpm pumper. On the right is a 1934 Chevrolet with a front-mounted pump. After World War II, the USA apparatus was sold to local fire departments, many of them volunteer. Credit: Fred Crismon.

Jamesport, Long Island, New York used this 1939 Walter pumper. Walters were all-wheel-drive chassis and frequently were used for snowplows. Credit: Bob Schierle.

While not a volunteer rig, this is an example of a commercial truck, probably school bus, chassis used for a ladder truck. The chassis is an early 1930 White Model 63 which was equipped by Pirsch for use in Grand Island, Nebraska. It has a small booster tank and pump. The second picture is of a postcard, and it shows this rig on the right. Also shown are a Stutz pumper, a Chevrolet chief's buggy, and, to the far left, a fire department training tower. Credit: Stuhr Museum of the Prairie Pioneer.

North Brunswick, New Jersey's 1939 White Super Power 500-gpm pumper built by Pirsch. Credit: Bill Schwartz.

At the scenes of multiple-alarm fires, canteen trucks appear to feed the fire fighters, serving them coffee, cool drinks, and sandwiches. The canteen, on a 1930 White 60 chassis, was operated by the fire department in Camden, New Jersey. More recently the task has been taken over by volunteer groups such as, the Salvation Army, which operates its own trucks, or local fire buff groups. Credit: Volvo/White.

Volunteer FIREMEN Notice This Electric SIREN

Complete $8 55 EACH

Drives from your regular six-volt battery. It attaches to the motor and is out of sight. The Air-turbine is 4 inches in diameter and turns over at 7,200 R.P.M. It is the MOST EFFECTIVE Warning Signal on the road.

The Illustrated model is for Country use on Cars and fast Trucks and Busses. It should not be used in Cities where Fire apparatus is Siren equipped. But for country use it ends that being held up for miles by a load of hay, a wide van with a deaf driver lighted with moonshine. You touch your Siren button and AS THEY MOVE OVER, YOU SHOOT BY! TRY IT!

Volunteer Members who have their own private cars and use them when responding to alarms should be equipped with this Siren to clear the road and distinguish their cars from all other vehicles.

Every Fire Chief should call the attention of Volunteer Members to this and the very special low price at which we are offering these Sirens.

It is the most compact Siren we have ever seen, takes up but little room inside the hood or on the running board or in front of the radiator. Shipping weight, complete, only 5 lbs.

No. B615. Siren Horn, Complete, with Bracket, $8 55 all wiring and Button, each..................

7

This Darley catalog advertisement is for a siren for volunteer firemen to place on their own autos. Credit: W.S. Darley.

This page from a W.S. Darley catalog in the mid-1930s shows how their equipment was used for "home-built" rigs throughout the country. Credit: W.S. Darley.

Chapter 5
1941-1950

This was an eventful decade. War in Europe had started in 1939, and, after Pearl Harbor, the United States was engaged in war on both sides of the world. During 1940, the Germans bombed London intensively, and there was considerable fear that "it could happen here." Air raid and blackout drills were held in cities throughout the country. An elaborate volunteer civil defense effort was set up and included auxiliary police and fire units, as well as air raid wardens. Espionage and sabotage were also feared; and many industrial plants formed their own fire brigades and equipped a truck to carry fire-fighting gear. Equipment was scarce and, for the most part, the civil defense fire fighters were expected to aid the regulars at the fire scene.

An article published three weeks after Pearl Harbor described the fire-fighting auxiliaries in New York City. They received regular fire-fighting training and could "identify a poison gas, call a bomb by its right name, and know how to render both ineffective."[1] The equipment to be used had not arrived; it was to be mounted on small trailers, stored throughout the city and then towed by an auto where needed. Trailers in this type of service had welded steel bodies and pneumatic tires. One man could push a trailer and fasten it to the rear bumper of the nearest available auto. Most trailers carried about 500 feet of 1-1/2-inch hose, along with an adapter, to permit reduction from the standard fireplug outlet. Each trailer carried the hose plus hose spanner, hydrant wrench, 16-foot ladder in eight-foot sections, six flashlights, axe, pike pole, New York-type bar for forcible entry, first-aid kit, red lantern, 12 steel helmets, three buckets of sand and a long-handled shovel (for incendiary bomb fires), and an Indian backpack fire pump. In some areas, the trailers also carried a small pump and some suction hose.

In April 1942, the village board in Iola, Wisconsin voted to purchase new fire-fighting equipment. They spent $350 for a used 1938 Reo 1-1/2-ton truck purchased in Milwaukee. To equip this truck, they spent an additional $300 for a new centrifugal pump, 100 feet of new booster line hose, a used reel for hose, a new power-takeoff, two new power shut-off valves, a new pressure gauge, and a used nozzle.[2]

In many communities, women now joined the ranks of volunteer and auxiliary fire fighters. An article about the volunteer "fire ladies" in Ashville, New York told of their being organized during the war. Some female volunteers remained after the war (and they were needed in postwar suburbs because, during daytime, men were working in the central city). The article also contained an observation that reflects on male chauvinism of the time: "Since Ashville's Peter Pirsch pumper is used exclusively by the men, the ladies drive a truck built on a Chevrolet chassis and equipped to carry a pump and 500 gallons of water."[3]

---

*1. Dickey Meyer, "Citizen-Firemen," **New York Times Magazine** (Dec. 28, 1941), page 13.*

*2. Janneyne Gnacinski, **Iola Fire Department Centennial** (Iola: Iola Historical Society, 1992), page 11.*

*3. "Ashville Fire Ladies Protect Our Community," **The American City** (June 1946), page 7.*

The military gained considerable experience using high-pressure fog to fight fires, especially aboard ships. After the war, fog equipment, which made much better use of a limited water supply and also reduced water damage, began appearing on civilian fire-fighting equipment. In 1947, Coalinga, California bought a White with a high-pressure fog pump. "The little White ... put out over 90% of Coalinga's fires for the next twenty years."[4]

A 1949 movie was released, called "Impact," and it starred Brian Donlevy. As part of the story, he took refuge in a small town named Larkspur in Idaho. That segment was actually filmed in Larkspur, California, a suburb of San Francisco. As evidence of his becoming a part of his new home community, the hero became a volunteer fireman and was shown joining with other volunteers in responding to a call. The Larkspur firehouse and the volunteers' American LaFrance pumper were shown in the movie, and the scene was a real slice of Americana. The "real" Larkspur volunteers raised money for many years by running a dance bowl.

A siren, and then an airhorn, replaced the fire bell in Los Gatos, California, which had served since 1899. The bell was removed, along with its 60-foot tower. This structure was then moved to a restaurant near Lodi, California, where the owner had constructed a large chicken perched on the tower's top as a tourist draw. (Later, the bell was returned to Los Gatos to a more dignified setting, and may be seen today in the Los Gatos town plaza.)

A few miles south of Los Gatos, the Alma Fire Protection District was organized about 1950. The district's first apparatus was a 1941 Autocar 1700-gallon gasoline tanker converted to fire use with a 350-gpm pump. It was quartered with the Santa Clara County Ranger Unit of the California Department of Forestry & Fire Protection. In the same vicinity, the Redwood Estates Volunteer Fire Department came into existence in 1949 when a delegation of Redwood Estates residents made a bid of $400 for an old forestry service truck.

In 1947, 27 volunteer fire fighters were killed in the Texas City blast. "Three of the volunteer force of 30 were sick or out of town. At the first alarm, the others responded to a man and were the first to drag their hoses into the burning French freighter that touched off the tragedy. Within half an hour, every one of them was dead."[5]

Wartime experience with all-wheel drive vehicles was responsible for some new equipment for fire-fighting rigs. Both the Jeep and the Dodge Power Wagon date from World War II. War surplus trucks also became available, and many rural departments used them for building tankers. (Even today, surplus military equipment is made available to states, and some outfit it for forest fire-fighting, then house the rigs in local stations.) At the war's end, the military also sold its surplus of conventional fire engines that it had purchased during the war to protect bases and production plants.

After the war, new truck sales resumed. Models looked like the 1942 versions but with chrome trim. In about 1948, most truck makes came out with their new postwar designs. Regular truck sales climbed to 1.3 million in 1950. In the years following the war, a number of improvements on commercial trucks were introduced. They included the hydraulic seat, under-the-hood light, alternators, semi-automatic transmissions, hydraulic liftgates, variable-pitch cooling fans, power steering, sanders (in front of driving wheels), and tilt cabs. Many departments installed two-way radios for dispatching and communicating with fire trucks.

---

4. *Oil But No Water, a History of the Coalinga Fire Department* (Coalinga, CA: the Fire Department, ca. 1980), page 42.
5. *Nation's Business* (October 1948), page 36.

Plant employees often manned their company's fire apparatus. Here's a late '40s American LaFrance pumper, used by the A.E. Staley Company, carrying a large number of fire fighters. This was a custom rig and marked the move in custom apparatus design toward placing the driver's seat ahead of the power plant. Credit: A.E. Staley Manufacturing Company.

Scotts Valley, California built this 1942 Model U-70 Autocar with Heil Tank into a 1600-gallon tanker with a 750-gpm pump mounted in the rear of the apparatus. Credit: Wayne Sorensen Collection.

Clifton Park, New York, used this 1941 Chevrolet with a 500-gpm Barton American pump. Note the suction inlet is in a hole in the cab door. Credit: Dick Adelman.

Seagrave used a 1941 Chevrolet chassis to build a 500-gpm triple-combination for Emmett, Idaho. Credit: Wayne Sorensen.

Many fire departments operate emergency units. Grand Island, Nebraska operated this rig on a 1941 Chevrolet chassis. It carried an iron lung which moved on rails. (This was in an era when some polio victims were confined to iron lungs to support their breathing.) It also carried a resuscitator, two inhalators and two cots. Credit: Motor Vehicle Manufacturers Association.

An ambulance body on a 1941 Chevrolet panel was later converted for use for the Loudon Township Volunteer Fire Department in Kilgore, Ohio. On the side one can see racks for holding the ladder and a hose reel at the rear. Credit: E. Aderer.

This 1942 Chevrolet was used by the volunteer fire company in Farmington, Delaware. It looks like a converted oil tank truck to which a front-mounted pump and an overhead ladder rack have been added. Credit: Ray Stevens.

The Chickasaw Village Fire Department in Tennessee used this Oren-outfitted 1942 Chevrolet with a 500-gpm pump. Note the lack of chrome and long, preconnected suction hose. Credit: Dick Adelman.

The Fisherville Volunteer Fire Department, in Tennessee, used this ex-military 1942-43 Chevrolet. Part of the grille has been cut away to hold a 300-gpm Darley front-mount pump. Credit: Dick Adelman.

A 1942 Chevrolet World War II military Model 110 QMC 4X4 chassis with front-mounted pump used by Rockleigh, New Jersey. Credit: Wayne Sorensen Collection.

West LaFayette, Ohio used this 1946 Chevrolet which had been outfitted by Darley. Credit: John F. Sytsma.

Close-up of pump control panel on a 1946 Chevrolet/Oren, sold by the New Jersey Fire Equipment Company as "Great Eastern Fire Apparatus." The rig was delivered in 1946 to Folsom, New Jersey. It had a 500-gpm pump. Credit: Ernest M. Day.

Lambs Terrace, New Jersey's fire department must have wanted to flaunt its exclusiveness; the sign at the rear of this 1946 Chevrolet tanker says, "For members only." Credit: Ernest N. Day.

Bartlett, Tennessee used this 1949 Chevrolet outfitted by Central Fire Truck Corporation of St. Louis and Manchester, Missouri. It carried 400 gallons of water and had a 500-gpm pump. Credit: Dick Adelman.

A 1947 Chevrolet COE used to build a rescue truck for service in Maui, Hawaii. It has a large winch in front. The body is made of wood. Credit: Dick Adelman.

The Boardman Company used this 1950 Chevrolet chassis to build a triple-combination. Note floodlight on the roof. The rig was for the Meade Fire Department in Kansas. Credit: The Boardman Company.

This Chevrolet COE, circa 1950, was originally a petroleum tanker; it was converted by volunteers in Jeffersonville, Kentucky into a fire tanker, carrying 1200 gallons of water. A PTO-driven pump produced 250 gpm. Credit: Dick Adelman.

Corbitt Company built the 1950 chassis for this 750-gpm triple-combination mounted by the Oren-Roanoke Corporation of Roanoke, Virginia for Chesapeake City, Maryland. Credit: Dick Adelman.

This 1941 Challenger was built in Sacramento with a 1000-gpm pump and 350-gallon water tank on a Diamond T chassis for Milbrae, California. Credit: Wayne Sorensen.

A 1942 Diamond T chassis was used by Pirsch to build this heavily laden quad for Deepwater, New Jersey. Credit: Bill Schwartz.

A 1946 Diamond T chassis was used by Coast Inc. to mount a 500-gpm triple-combination for Wells, Nevada. The rig was also equipped with a high pressure pump. Credit: Milton G. Sorensen.

Diamond T trucks were probably the most attractive commercial trucks marketed during the period 1935-1950 and many were used to mount fire-fighting bodies. This is a 1949 Diamond T model 509 SCH chassis, and our guess is that "SCH" meant that it was intended for school buses. This one became a city service truck outfitted by Seagrave for the Cape Elizabeth Fire Department. Credit: Seagrave/FWD.

A 1941 Dodge-Fabco 500-gpm triple-combination on the left drafts water from the 1949 White tractor/trailer with a 2000 gallon tank. The tanker has a 500-gpm pump at the rear. These rigs were in service with the Santa Clara County Central Fire District. Credit: Wayne Sorensen Collection.

Atascadero, California's 1946 Dodge Light Wagon built by Van Pelt Inc. of Oakdale, California. Credit: Wayne Sorensen.

An order of pumpers by FABCO, an apparatus builder in the San Francisco Bay Area, were built on Dodge chassis for the U.S. Army during World War II. Credit: FABCO.

A 1945 Dodge outfitted by Darley was used in Hurley, Wisconsin. Credit: W.S. Darley & Company.

General of Detroit built this body on a 1946 Dodge chassis for Vienna, West Virginia. Credit: National Automotive History Collection, Detroit Public Library.

Kuna, Idaho's 1946 Dodge triple-combination has a 250-gpm front-mounted pump. The rig looks homemade. Credit: Wayne Sorensen.

A 1950 Dodge 4X4 brush rig used by Sand Lake, Alaska, was probably built on a surplus military truck. Credit: Wayne Sorensen.

Thousands of Ford 1-1/2-ton 4X2 chassis were used in the 1940s as the basis for low-cost fire apparatus, and the armed forces bought its share. The Ward LaFrance Truck Corporation of Elmira Heights, New York built this 500-gpm pumper, and it saw service at the U.S. Army Arsenal at Milan, Tennessee. After its army service, it was put into civilian service at Atwood, Tennessee. Credit: Dick Adelman.

While not a volunteer rig, the tractor pulling this tillered aerial trailer is a Federal from the late 1940s. It's parked in front of a Federal dealership in New Jersey. Credit: Mort Glasofer.

While these are chassis from the 1930s, they are included in this chapter because they were converted to auxiliary fire apparatus during World War II. This photo was taken at the 1944 centennial parade in Kokomo, Indiana. It shows two rigs built for use by the Civil Defense Auxiliary. In the front we see a 1937 Ford with a separate engine and pump mounted to the rear of the cab. In the rear stand two women and two men, all wearing civil defense helmets. "Continental Steel Corp." is painted on the door. Behind it is a mid-'30s Dodge with "City of Kokomo" painted on the door. It also carries a pump, plus ladders and suction hose in an overhead rack. Headlights have been painted over, leaving a narrow slit for use under blackout conditions. (During World War II, blackouts were practiced throughout the United States.) Credit: Howard County Historical Museum.

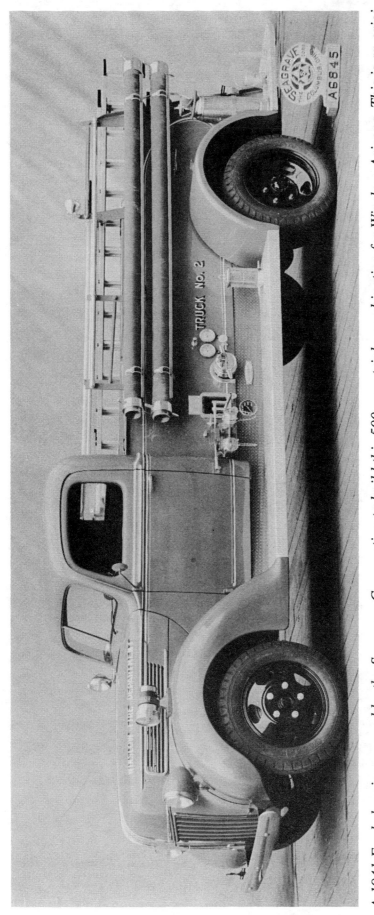

A 1941 Ford chassis was used by the Seagrave Corporation to build this 500-gpm triple-combination for Winslow, Arizona. This is an original factory photo; the little Seagrave sign at the right shows the job order number for this chassis, A 6845. Credit: Seagrave.

The Community Fire Company of Trumbaversville, Pennsylvania used this 1942 Ford V-8 with an 85 hp engine and 500-gpm triple-combination body. Credit: Jim Burner.

The Oren-Roanoke Corporation of Roanoke, Virginia used a 1942 Ford chassis to build this 500-gpm triple-combination rig for Chickasaw Village, Tennessee. The suction hose is carried around the front of the rig. Credit: Dick Adelman.

This 1946 Ford-American LaFrance was once used in Lake Grove, California and is currently owned by Ken Bechthold. Close-up shows pump panel on driver's side. Credit: Don Wood.

The volunteer fire company in Mars, Pennsylvania purchased this Darley rig built on a 1946 Ford school bus chassis. It had a 600-gpm pump and a 300- gallon booster tank. Inside were bench seats, apparently to carry members to fires in situations where they reported to the station after the first rig had left. Possibly the bench seats were also used during parades. Credit: W.S. Darley.

Oren-Roanoke Corporation used a 1947 Ford chassis for this 500-gpm front-mount pump with large crew cab for Bedford Road, Maryland. The striping pattern was a left-over from the 1930s when trucks were painted this way to match the sweeping curves of streamlined auto fenders. Credit: Dick Adelman.

The Fire Fighter Truck Company of Rock Island, Illinois used a 1949 Ford F-7 chassis and front-mounted pump to build a pumper for the "Volunteer Fire Dept. Inc." of Troy Township in Illinois. Credit: Dan G. Martin.

American LaFrance mounted this tanker body on a 1949 Ford chassis. Credit: American LaFrance.

The state hospital at North Warren, Pennsylvania used a 1950 Ford C-800 COE tractor with front-mounted pump to pull their shop-built service ladder trailer. Credit: Roland Boulet.

Boardman Company used this 1950 Ford F-7 chassis to build a 500-gpm pumper for Bentonville, Arkansas. Credit: The Boardman Company.

A 1940s FWD used by Dupont and Larabee Townships and the City of Marion, Wisconsin. The sign on the door lists the three and adds "community engine." Credit: FWD.

A 1946 FWD pumper with overhead ladder racks. Credit: FWD.

Rabbit Creek, Alaska used this World War II surplus gasoline truck to build a tanker for its volunteer fire department. The chassis was a GMC-CCKW 6X6. The cab has been enclosed. Credit: Wayne Sorensen.

W.S. Darley of Chicago built this 500-gpm pumper on a 1948 GMC chassis for Golden, Colorado. Note elaborate striping. Credit: Dick Adelman.

Volunteers in Eastport, Maryland operated this ex-U.S. Navy Type FFN-3 1943 International-John Bean high pressure pumper.

This 1943 International was originally built for use by the Canadian Air Force. Later it was converted into a tanker for use by the St. Stephen Fire Department in New Brunswick. Credit: Roy Fobes.

The volunteer fire company in Marmora, New Jersey used this 1944 International flat-bed. A 500-gpm skid pump is carried behind the cab, and a 500-gallon water tank is on the truck bed. Credit: Jim Burner.

Cordova's volunteer firemen's association in Maryland had an early crew cab on a 1946 International K Series 500-gpm triple-combination. Credit: Ray Stevens.

A 1948 International with bodywork by Task Master Equipment Company is equipped with a 250-gpm Hale pump and 250-gallon water tank. It was built for Washington Fire Company No. 1 of Ocean Grove, New Jersey.

Van Pelt used a 1949 International K Series to build Atascadero, California's 750-gpm pumper with a 500-gallon water tank. Credit: Wayne Sorensen.

A group of 172 farmers in Tama County, Iowa chipped in to buy this 1950 International rig. Credit: State Historical Society of Iowa.

Ex-World War II jeep has a fire plow used for fighting grass and forest fires. Note hose coil on the hood. The rig also has a drop-in pump tank and a brush guard. Shovels are stacked between front seats. Credit: South Carolina Forestry Commission.

A 1948 jeep has a body and pump installed by Howe Fire Apparatus Company. The rig has a 400-gpm Barton front-mounted pump and overhead ladders. It was purchased by the East End Volunteer Fire Company of Many, Louisiana. Credit: Wayne Sorensen.

A late '40s Kenworth with its newly installed pump is being tested. The suction hose takes water from the same pit into which outlet hoses are discharging. Credit: Paccar.

In 1946, the Ahrens-Fox Fire Engine Company of Cincinnati built Warrenton, Virginia's 500-gpm centrifugal pumper on a LeBlond-Schacht Truck Company chassis. Credit: Ahrens-Fox.

A wartime model (no chrome) 1944 Mack L Series 1000-gpm triple-combination was used by Livermore, California. Credit: Paul Darrel.

General of Detroit used a 1948 Mack chassis to build a squad car for Curwensville, Pennsylvania. Credit: General of Detroit and Dick Adelman.

A 1950 Reo M 34 ex-military chassis was used to build this 2-1/2 ton tanker for Cedar Top, Pennsylvania. Credit: Jim Burner Jr.

A 1948 Studebaker M Series chassis was used by Pirsch to build this 200-gpm pumper with 250-gallon water tank for Hooper, Nebraska. Credit: Peter Pirsch and Sons and Dick Adelman.

Surplus "custom" rigs were sometimes sold to volunteer departments. Ward LaFrance Truck Corporation of Elmira Heights, New York built this 750-gpm pumper for the U.S. Navy in 1950. When it became surplus, it was purchased for use by Monterey County, California volunteers. Credit: Wayne Sorensen.

San Carlos, California purchased this 500-gpm pumper from Van Pelt with a "squirrel tail" suction carried over the front of the 1941 White. It carries floodlights. Alongside are helmets and turn-out gear. Credit: John Graham.

Workers with other assignments were sometimes expected to fight or assist in the fighting of fires. This rig, on a 1941 White 820 tractor chassis, was used in New York tunnels as a wrecker/recovery vehicle. It could function in either direction without needing to turn around. Of interest to us is the foam hopper and coiled hose, shown between the two wheels. Foam powder, carried in five-gallon tins in the truck bed, was fed through the hopper into the stream of water. This was used to fight gasoline fires and also was spread over gasoline and oil at the accident site. Credit: Volvo/White.

As part of the civil defense efforts during World War II, civilians were organized into volunteer fire-fighting groups. This 1943 photo shows a White Horse step van used by civil defense fire fighters in San Francisco. The van carries ladders and a suction hose on the roof, but we see no evidence of a pump. It probably ran with regular rigs. Credit: Volvo-White.

The Live Oak Fire Protection District near Santa Cruz, California used this 1947 White-Van Pelt 500-gpm triple-combination. Credit: Wayne Sorensen.

A white White, a 1948 model WA 22 with a quad body, was used by the Community Volunteer Fire Company of New Brunswick, New Jersey. At the rear one can see ends of ladders and suction hose. Several floodlights are carried. Credit: Volvo White.

The Approval Fire Equipment Company of Rockville Center, New York mounted this emergency body on a 1948 COE White chassis for the volunteers' department in Loyalsock, Pennsylvania. Credit: John J. Robrecht.

Van Pelt Inc. used a 1948 White Super Power chassis for Union City, California's 500-gpm pumper. Credit: Wayne Sorensen.

A 1948 White COE chassis was used by Van Pelt to built a 350-gpm front-mount 1000-gallon tanker for Ben Lomond, California. Credit: Wayne Sorensen.

Commercial rigs usually carried nameplates of both the chassis manufacturer and the apparatus outfitter. This White, from the 1940s, had a Van Pelt emblem placed on the side of the hood. Credit: Don Wood.

Finishing the gold lettering on the side of an early '30s pumper in the Procter Keefe Body Company in Detroit. Credit: Motor Vehicle Manufacturers Association.

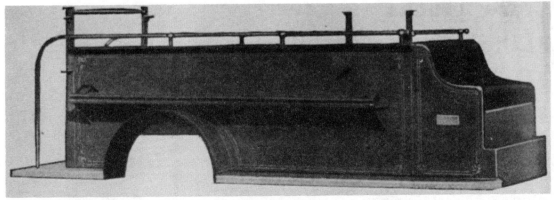

W.S. Darley advertised this hose body in their catalog. It fit most chassis makes and was finished with a prime coat. Credit: W.S. Darley.

On Oct. 4, 1948, this postage stamp was issued honoring the 300th anniversary of volunteer firemen in the United States. The stamp was first issued in Dover, Delaware.

Chapter 6
1951-1960

An article in *Life* magazine pictured the volunteer fire department in Franklin Village, Michigan, a suburb of Detroit, noting that its roster included eight company presidents, plus many other professionals. After the suburb became fashionable with commuters, these residents found that it was poorly protected from fires. "The new homeowners raised money for equipment, wheedled more through connections, and now have a crack $180,000 plant. They man the trucks themselves, responding to alarms relayed by a telephone and radio system to their plants and offices all over the area. Those downtown race up the Lodge Expressway."[1]

An article in the *BFG Merchandiser*, published for Goodrich dealers, noted the feats of one of its hose dealers, Ernest N. Day, of the New Jersey Fire Equipment Company headquartered in Dunellen. Day had started selling fire-fighting supplies in 1930 and formed his own company in 1933. In addition to selling hose, the company also sold Pirsch apparatus. "Today [1955] New Jersey Equipment Corporation is delivering between 30 and 40 engines a year, including aerial ladders to most of the big cities in the East at a cost of about $36,000 each." A picture showed a new pumper on a commercial chassis being loaded with B.F. Goodrich Dacron fire hose at the firm's facility. (This information was supplied by Mr. Day, who, in a 1992 letter to the authors, said that his firm had sold over 1,200 rigs, 90 percent of which went to volunteer departments.)

On conventional trucks during this decade, automatic transmissions became available, especially for small and medium-sized models. Plastics were used for many interior fittings. Fiberglass was used in some cabs. Aluminum engine parts reduced the truck's overall weight. The Army started using 2-1/2-ton trucks with automatic transmissions. One reason given for this was that many G.I.s didn't know how to shift. Air brakes and power steering became common on larger rigs. So did tubeless tires, although many truckers continued to prefer tubes. A few makes of trucks used air suspension, and others used rubber cushion suspension. Tilt cabs became very common and were used for many cab-over-engine models. Locking differentials came into use. Gas turbine engines were tested on trucks. V-8 engines became more popular on autos, and soon were available for most makes of trucks. V-8 engines were shorter than in-line versions, which meant the cab could be moved forward. Use of diesels was widespread.

The Redwood Estates Volunteer Fire Department, near Los Gatos, California, in 1959 made their second purchase of apparatus, an old gasoline tanker remodeled into a combination tanker and pumper. The volunteers in nearby Alma backed up the Redwood Volunteers. Support for the volunteers came from an annual dance and barbecue. Nearby, in Campbell, the department now had a paid fire chief and eight full-time paid firemen.

---

1. Life (April 25, 1960), page 65.

There were three changes in custom apparatus which would subsequently influence the design of commercial apparatus as well. The first was the placement of the driver's seat at the very front of the rig, ahead of the engine. In addition, seating was supplied for other fire fighters. The other two changes were aerial ladders mounted at the rear and snorkels, which were elevated fire-fighting platforms.

A.L. Hansen Manufacturing Company supplied hardware to truck body builders. Here, in one of their catalogs from about 1950, they indicate that they supplied several items of hardware to the General Body Company of Chicago, which used the hardware to build this rig on an Autocar COE chassis. Credit: A.L. Hansen.

A 1951 Chevrolet/Pirsch 500-gpm combination was used in Stevens, Pennsylvania. Credit: Roland Boulet.

Approved Fire Equipment Company of Rockville Center, New York followed the Ahrens-Fox cab forward design on a C.D. Beck chassis to build a 1000-gpm triple-combination for Glenwood Landing, New York, in 1957. Mack's Fire Apparatus Division adapted the cab forward design to build their C-85 model when Mack acquired Beck in the fall of 1956. Credit: Jim Burner.

Street flushers had large water tanks and pump mechanisms for spraying water. Many served as a reserve tanker for their local fire department. This rig, on a 1952 Autocar COE chassis, was built for the Port of New York Tunnel Authority and was used for flushing tunnels. Front sweep nozzles are below the headlights, and the rack at the rear holds nozzles for spraying top and sides. The truck had a 500-gpm Champion pump. Information supplied by Autocar to its dealers said the rig "can also be used as auxiliary fire fighting pumping unit." Credit: Volvo/White.

A 1953 Autocar was outfitted as a pumper by Boyer for use by the Hockessin Volunteer Fire Company in Delaware. Credit: Volvo White.

The East Whiteland Fire Association in Chester County, Pennsylvania used this 1954 Autocar with a Hale 750-gpm pump. It carried 1500 feet of 2-1/2-inch hose, 500 feet of 1-1/2 inch hose and a 750-gallon water tank. The pump was enclosed inside the compartment. Note "W" in front bumper. Credit: Volvo/White.

Spring Lake Heights, New Jersey purchased this 750-gpm triple-combination from Oren-Roanoke Corporation of Roanoke, Virginia on a 1957 chassis built by the Available Truck Company of Chicago. Credit: Dick Adelman.

Nelson Equipment Company used a 1951 Chevrolet chassis to mount this 500-gpm triple-combination for Shoshone County, Idaho. Credit: Wayne Sorensen Collection.

A 1954 Chevrolet Series 3600 Model HR Rescue Squad of Pacifica, California. Credit: Wayne Sorensen Collection.

This late '50s tanker on a Chevrolet chassis carries this wording on back of the tank: "Luverne Tanker Fire Truck mfg'd by the Luverne Fire Apparatus Co., of Luverne, Minnesota." It was probably displayed at some trade shows and then sold. It carries a small midship pump plus a second, portable pump at the rear. The portable pump could be placed in areas that the truck couldn't reach and be used to either fight the blaze or to fill the truck's tank. Credit: Hannay Reels.

A 1957 Chevrolet cab-forward outfitted as a quint by General Safety for Menomonie, Wisconsin. Its pump was rated at 750-gpm and its aerial ladder was 65 feet long. Credit: Dan G. Martin.

The Rockaway County Beach Volunteer Fire Department, in Baltimore County, Maryland, used this 1959 Chevrolet Spartan with an American LaFrance pumper. Credit: American LaFrance.

Oren-Roanoke used a 1955 Corbitt chassis built in Henderson, North Carolina to build a 750-gpm triple-combination for Moonachie, New Jersey. Credit: John Sytsma.

Wildwood, New Jersey had the Oren-Roanoke Corporation build this 750-gpm triple-combination on a Corbitt chassis. Credit: Jim Burner.

Van Pelt used a 1952 Diamond T chassis to build this 500-gpm combination for the Agnew State Hospital located in Santa Clara County, California. Credit: Wayne Sorensen.

This 1951 photo shows volunteer firemen in Granger, Iowa testing a new Dodge rig that was paid for by donations from residents of Granger. Credit: State Historical Society of Iowa.

This 1952 Dodge Power Wagon was outfitted by Coast with a 300-gpm PTO-driven front-mounted pump and a 300-gallon tank. It was for use at the University of California's Radiation Laboratory. A radio antenna is tied down. Credit: University of California.

Several state forestry departments provide rural fire departments with converted military rigs to use in their own communities and be on call for forest fires. This '50s Dodge 4X4 ex-Army rig was outfitted by the Minnesota Department of Natural Resources for use by the Forada Fire Department. In the rear we see a slip-on pump, a self-contained combination of pump, water tank, and hose reel that can be transferred from truck to truck. Credit: Minnesota DNR.

Panaca, Nevada's 1955 Dodge 500-gpm triple-combination, mounted by L.N. Curtis & Sons of Oakland, California, displays bodywork by Heiser Body Company of Seattle, Washington. Credit: Heiser.

A 1958 Diamond T chassis was used by Roney of Portland, Oregon to build a 750-gpm triple combination with a 1000-gallon tank for Belfair, Washington. Credit: Bill Hattersley.

Morgan Hill, California's 1956 750-gpm Dodge-Van Pelt pumper is now painted yellow. Credit: Wayne Sorensen Collection.

A 1957 Dodge COE chassis was used by American LaFrance to build a 750-gpm triple-combination for Forest City, Illinois. Credit: Dick Adelman.

Central Fire Truck Corporation of St. Louis used this 1951 Duplex chassis to build a 750-gpm triple-combination for Dupo, Illinois. Credit: Dick Adelman.

A 1952 Federal 500-gpm triple-combination was used by the Independent Fire Company of Belford, New Jersey. Credit: Jim Burner.

The American Fire Apparatus Corporation of Battle Creek, Michigan used a 1951 Ford F-8 chassis with Marmon-Herrington all-wheel-drive to build a 500-gpm triple-combination for Ridge, Long Island, New York. Credit: Dan Martin.

This 1952 Ford F-2 pickup carried Battalion Chief #2 of the Santa Clara (California) County Central Fire District. Credit: Wayne Sorensen Collection.

The American Fire Apparatus Corporation of Battle Creek, Michigan used a 1952 Ford chassis and 500-gpm Barton front-mounted pump for the Volunteer Fire Company of Queen Anne-Hillsboro, Maryland. Credit: Dick Adelman.

Robeson Custom Fire Trucks is a branch of La Mesa Sheet Metal Works of La Mesa, California and both builds and rebuilds apparatus. Shown here were the firm's founders, George T. Robeson and Gene Robeson, in front of a 1953 Ford that they had just built for the La Mesa Fire Department. It had a 500-gallon booster tank and a 500-gpm Hale pump that had originally been a World War II surplus skid unit. Credit: Robeson.

Maxim Motor Company of Middelboro, Massachusetts built mostly custom apparatus on their own chassis. However, this 1953 Ford F-900 series chassis was used by them to build a 750-gpm triple-combination for Jonesboro, Arkansas. Credit: Dick Adelman.

Oren-Roanoke used a 1953 Ford F Series chassis to build a 500-gpm triple-combination for the Welcome Volunteer Fire Company of Oaklyn, New Jersey. Credit: Dick Adelman.

A 1953 Ford tanker used by the volunteer fire department in Moon Lake, Florida. It looks like an ex-oil company rig. Across the top of the tank is painted: "Neighbors Helping Neighbors." Credit: Elliot Kahn.

The Approval Fire Equipment Company of Rockville Center, New York used a 1955 Ford chassis to build this 500-gpm triple-combination for Pitman, New Jersey. Credit: Dick Adelman.

Adamsville, Tennessee purchased this 1956 Ford 500-gpm triple-combination from Central Fire Truck Corporation of St. Louis, Missouri. Credit: Dick Adelman.

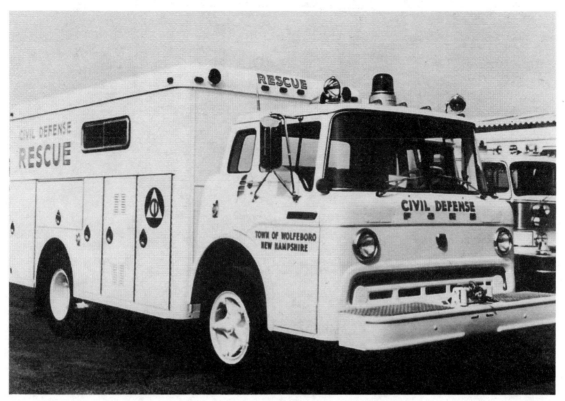

Ford C-series trucks such as this were introduced in 1957 and have the longest production run of any U. S. truck (including the Mack Bulldog). They have tilt cabs. This one, from the late '50s, was used by Gerstenslager Corporation to build a Civil Defense rescue truck for the Town of Wolfsboro, New Hampshire. Credit: Gerstenslager Corporation.

A 1958 Ford chassis was used by Howe Fire Apparatus Company to build this 750-gpm triple-combination for the Collister Fire District near Boise, Idaho. Credit: Wayne Sorensen.

The W.S. Darley Company of Chicago used this 1960 Ford C series chassis to build a 750-gpm triple-combination for the Cole Fire District near Boise, Idaho. Note the front pump mounted in front of the Ford tilt cab. Credit: W.S. Darley.

This 1951 FWD 750-gpm triple-combination was the fifth motor-driven fire rig used in Nevada City, California. The picture was taken just before the July 4th parade in 1980. Credit: Wayne Sorensen.

FWD delivered fire apparatus all over the United States. This 1951 500-gpm pumper was delivered to North York, Pennsylvania. Credit: John J. Robrecht.

FWD built this 1953 500-gpm triple-combination for Blair, Nebraska. Credit: Wayne Sorensen Collection.

Erwinna Pennsylvania's 1957 FWD 750-gpm triple-combination. Credit: Dick Adelman.

Wyoming, Michigan used this Pierce-outfitted snorkel carried on a late '50s FWD chassis. Credit: Pierce.

Brumbaugh Body Company of Altoona, Pennsylvania used a 1951 GMC chassis to build this 750-gpm pumper for the Parkland, Pennsylvania Fire Company. Note the row of hanging helmets. Credit: Dick Adelman.

A 1953 GMC-Van Pelt 1000-gpm triple-combination State of California Civil Defense pumper was assigned to the Santa Clara County Central Fire District. This was funded with a state/federal program that distributed apparatus throughout the state. Credit: Wayne Sorensen.

Food Machinery Corporation of San Jose, California built this 750-gpm pumper on a 1953 GMC 800 series chassis for the Cherryland Fire Protection District near Hayward, California. Credit: Paul Darrell.

The volunteers used a 1953 GMC Truck chassis and a 500-gpm skid pump for this triple-combination used in Eagle, Idaho. Credit: Wayne Sorensen.

This is Island Heights, New Jersey's 1954 GMC-TASC 750-gpm triple-combination. Credit: Jim Burner.

When C.D. Beck took over the assembly of Ahrens-Fox apparatus in 1954, an effort was made to promote a standard line of pumpers on commercial chassis. This 1954 triple-combination, built for Moonachie, New Jersey, was on a GMC chassis. Credit: Dick Adelman.

American LaFrance used a 1954 GMC chassis to build this rugged-looking 750-gpm pumper for Lexington, Tennessee. Credit: Dick Adelman.

Coast Apparatus built this 750-gpm triple-combination for Live Oak, in Sutter County, California, using a 1954 GMC chassis. Credit: Coast Apparatus.

American LaFrance used this mid-1950s GMC 550 chassis to build Boulder Creek, California a 750-gpm pumper. Credit: Wayne Sorensen.

A 1959 GMC chassis used by L.N. Curtis and Sons to build a 750-gpm triple-combination for Fallon Volunteer Fire Department in Nevada. Credit: L.N. Curtis.

An early '50s International 185 outfitted by Darley for use in the Hines Veterans Administration Hospital in Illinois. One can see that the Darley body began at the cowl. Credit: W.S. Darley.

American LaFrance built the pumper body on this early '50s International, used by Adam's Fire Department in Nashville, New York. The apparatus builder received the chassis with a complete cab. Credit: American LaFrance.

This 1951 International was outfitted by Coast with a 750-gpm midship pump and a triple-combination body for College Place, Washington. Note the location of the deck gun at the front of truck. Credit: Bill Hattersley.

American LaFrance used a 1959 International B series chassis to build this 750-gpm triple-combination for Mountain House, Idaho. It had a 500-gallon water tank. Credit: Wayne Sorensen.

In the 1950s, the Federal Office of Civil and Defense Mobilization provided some equipment that was used in civil disasters. Here are two views of a 1956 International panel truck and the equipment it carried for rescue work. Credit: U.S. Office of Civil and Defense Mobilization.

Approved Fire Apparatus of Rockville Center, New York built this rescue rig on an early '50s International chassis for Spring Valley, New York. Note how the warning lights are blended into the roof of the cab. Credit: Ernest M. Day.

Agnew State Hospital is located in Santa Clara County, California. The Coast Apparatus Company of Martinez, California used a 1960 International chassis to build this 500-gpm triple-combination for the hospital to use. The rig was operated by hospital staff when needed. Credit: Wayne Sorensen.

A 1960 International chassis was used by the Fire Apparatus Division of Crown Coach Corporation of Los Angeles to build this 750-gpm quint with a 50-foot Pitman Snorkel for Elko, Nevada. Credit: Wayne Sorensen.

A 1956 Jeep series chassis used by Darley to build this unit with a 500-gpm pump and 150-gallon water tank. Credit: W.S. Darley.

Howe Fire Apparatus Company used a 1958 Jeep FC-170 to build this triple-combination with front-mounted pump. Suction hose strainer is carried near headlight. Credit: Howe Fire Apparatus Company.

Gray Fire Apparatus of Lewiston, Idaho used a 1952 Kenworth chassis to build a 1000-gpm triple-combination for use in Lewiston. Credit: Wayne Sorensen.

A 1953 Kenworth chassis was used to build a 750-gpm triple-combination by Howard-Cooper of Seattle for Rockford, Washington. Credit: Bill Hattersley.

A 1959 Mack B-95 with semi-cab 1000-gpm purchased by Capitola, California. Later it was a muster rig for the Salsipuedes Fire Protection District. Credit: Wayne Sorensen.

This 1959 N series Mack sports a "Budd" cab almost identical in appearance to the Ford C Model. This rig was built for Westbury, Long Island, New York. Credit: Jim Burner.

A 1956 Peterbilt chassis was used by Coast Apparatus Inc. of Martinez, California to build this 1000-gpm open-seat pumper for the Burbank Fire District near San Jose. It was used later by Branciforte, California. Credit: Wayne Sorensen.

Marlboro, New Jersey ran this 1951 White outfitted by Oren-Roanoke. The rig had a 500-gpm pump. Note volunteers' helmets hanging alongside, with the chief's white helmet in front. Credit: Dick Adelman.

This 1957 photo shows a 1954 Reo used as a demonstrator by the Federal Civil Defense Administration. Most were placed with large, paid departments. Inventory of equipment carried is shown in the front of rig. Credit: Office of Civil and Defense Mobilization.

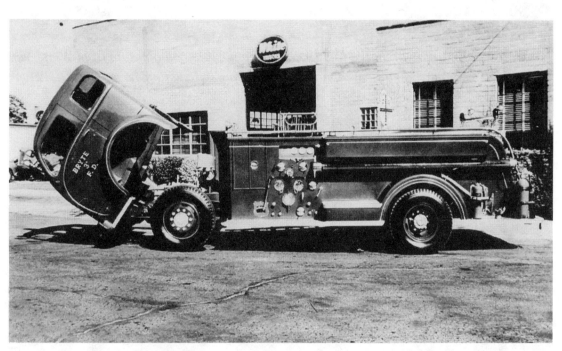

In 1949, White introduced the tilt cab, which could be raised easily to expose the engine and drivetrain. This 1951 model was outfitted by Van Pelt and was used by Bryte, California. Credit: Volvo/White.

Los Gatos, California purchased this 1951 750-gpm triple-combination from White-Van Pelt. It has a "squirrel tail" wraparound preconnected suction hose. Credit: Wayne Sorensen.

This 1952 White/Van Pelt 1000-gpm pumper was used in Samoa, California. Credit: Don Wood.

Quad body on a 1954 White 3022 chassis was used by the Thad Stevens volunteer fire department, Battle Creek, Michigan. Credit: Volvo/White.

W.S. Darley advertised this siren for summoning volunteers in their catalog. Credit: W.S. Darley.

The Schnabel Company of Pittsburgh, Pennsylvania built a number of rigs in the 1940s that had cushioned bench seats facing inward, inside the hose body, on which volunteers sat. We assume that they were used to carry volunteers from the station to the site of the fire, following the first engine out. They were also used for parades. Shown here are an International built for the Brentwood Volunteer Fire Company and a Diamond T built for Evans City. The Diamond T even had a canvas top for protection from the elements during parades. The Brentwood rig also carried two large flood lamps. Credit: Historical Society of Western Pennsylvania.

Chapter 7
1961-1970

An article in a 1968 issue of *The Reader's Digest* was about volunteer fire fighters, and contained the statement that of the nation's 24,000 fire departments, 22,000 depended upon volunteers. "Indeed half the nation's people now live in areas -- suburban, small-town and rural -- served by volunteer departments.... In all, the United States has more than one million volunteer firemen, as opposed to approximately 200,000 who are paid."[1] The article also indicated that whether a department was volunteer or paid did not, by itself, determine the community's fire insurance rating.

In a 1969 issue of *Popular Science*, an article indicated that there were 1,300,000 volunteer fire fighters in the United States compared with 200,000 full-time professionals. The article indicated that in Iowa, there were 852 different fire departments, but only 32 had paid members. The article further stated that the nation's volunteer departments were equipped with 84 million feet of 2-1/2-inch hose, 250,000 nozzles, 784,000 helmets, 575,000 turnout coats, and 500,000 pairs of protective gloves.[2] Equipment being purchased by many volunteer departments at this time include air and oxygen gear, walkie-talkie radios, resuscitators, portable floodlights, power tools, and foam generators. The article also reproduced an evaluation scale provided by *Fire Engineering Magazine* to evaluate the equipment needs of a community of 7000 with a volunteer department. The department should have:

1. Two or three fully equipped pumpers. A ladder truck was not needed unless there were tall buildings.
2. Thirty-five-foot truss-type ladders on the pumpers as well as 24-foot extension ladders.
3. Various nozzles, playpipes, fog nozzles and "Y" fittings.
4. Six fire brooms and backpack tank extinguishers.
5. A portable pump on pumpers for use where trucks can't reach surface water supplies.
6. Foam generating equipment on one pumper.
7. One portable electric generator and floodlights.
8. One smoke ejector.
9. A helmet, boots, and fire coat for each volunteer.
10. First aid kit on each pumper.
11. One resuscitator.
12. Breathing equipment.
13. Two-way radios on every piece of equipment.
14. Two walkie-talkies.
15. Two salvage covers, mops, brooms, and squeegees.

---

1. James Daniel, *"How Good Are Our Volunteer Firemen?"* **The Reader's Digest** *(June 1968), page 120.*
2. **Popular Science** *(May 1969), page 96.*

In Black River Falls, Wisconsin, a road and property numbering system for rural areas was completed, and a guide for babysitters dealing with fire dangers was distributed. In Iola, Wisconsin, a former milk tanker on an International chassis was purchased and converted for fire-fighting use by volunteers working evenings in the Rice Auto Body Shop. In 1962, in Nevada City, California, the fire bell was replaced by an airhorn. The bell (which still can be seen on top of city hall) was hard to hear compared to the air horn. The horn was coded to indicate the location of the fire.

In 1961, the Santa Clara County Central Fire Protection District volunteer division operated two stations. One was located in Almaden with a 1948 White-Van Pelt 500-gpm triple-combination. This unit responded 18 times during that year. In the 1960s, the Los Gatos, California fire department went from being all-volunteer to becoming a paid fire-fighting force, supplemented by volunteers. Neighboring Saratoga moved to using paid fire fighters in 1966. The town of Los Gatos was operating three stations at the time it decided to merge with the Santa Clara County Central Fire District on May 1, 1970. In this same decade, the Alma Fire Protection District (also now part of Santa Clara County Central Fire Protection District) had purchased its second piece of apparatus, a 750-gpm pumper with a 600-gallon water tank mounted on a 1967 Ford C series chassis by Van Pelt.

Recognizing the increasing popularity of cab-ahead apparatus, International introduced its CO-8190 chassis in the mid-1960s. The driver and two fire fighters sat ahead of the engine. Behind them was a seat on each side for additional fire fighters. It was available with 164-inch and 228-inch wheelbases and came with either single or dual rear axles. The shorter wheelbase could turn at a 35-degree angle inside a radius of 32 feet. A low-profile design accommodated placement of ladders overhead. It came with two engine options, both V-8s. The 234-hp engine could drive a 1000-gpm pump, and the 285-hp engine could drive a 1500-gpm pump. Engines, metered cooling systems, and lubrication systems were designed for sustained periods of pumping. Sales literature said:

"You can also customize this production model with numerous factory-installed options. These include dual ignition, special wheelbases, open-top cab, oversize alternator and batteries, tinted glass, air or hydraulic brakes, power steering as regular production line options. Even automatic transmission and other special features are available.

"Add the features offered by the equipment manufacturer and [fire apparatus] body builder, and your new CO-8190 will be the finest fire truck you can buy."[3]

Truck and bus sales in 1970 were 1.7 million units. Some of the increase in truck sales was due to light pickup trucks being bought by individuals and used for their personal transportation. Truck registrations in 1970 were 19 million, plus nearly 400,000 buses. Emission control devices were being added to combat air pollution.

3. *International Fire Truck Chassis* (Chicago: International Harvester Company, ca. 1965), page 3.

This 1962 Chevrolet pickup has body modifications by Gerstenslager Corporation of Wooster, Ohio. There are several doors to equipment compartments on the side. Credit: Gerstenslager Corporation.

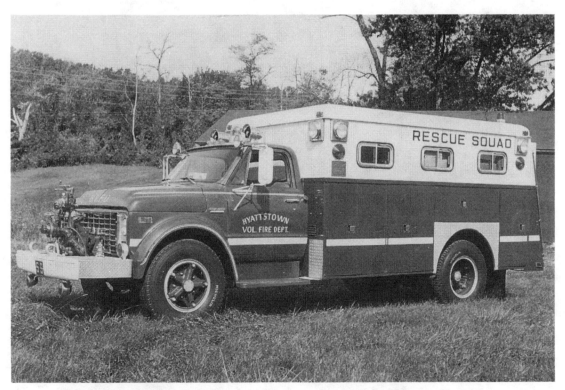

A 1962 Chevrolet 60 Series chassis was used to build a rescue squad with a 750-gpm pump for Hyattstown, Maryland. Rescue squads with front-mounted pumps are rare. Builder is unknown. Credit: Dick Adelman.

A 1963 Chevrolet COE tilt cab was used by the Economy Volunteer Fire Department of Beaver County, Pennsylvania. The pumper's body was by Ward LaFrance. Credit: Ward LaFrance.

This is a 1964 Chevrolet van used by Haney to build a rescue unit for the volunteer fire department in Maple Ridge, British Columbia. Credit: Bill Hattersley.

A 1965 Chevrolet step van built into a rescue van by Billings, Montana. Note axes carried below the windshield. Credit: Bill Friedrick.

Two views of a Gerstenslager rescue body on a mid-'60s Chevrolet COE with a short wheelbase chassis. Credit: Gerstenslager Corporation.

A camper body with an extended roof became an emergency vehicle on a 1968 Chevrolet chassis. The truck had all-wheel drive. Credit: Gerstenslager Corporation.

Wesco Fire Division, Industrial Steel Tank and Body Works, of Los Angeles used a 1964 Diamond T chassis to build a 1000-gpm triple-combination for Sunnyvale, California. Credit: Wayne Sorensen.

Seagrave used a 1961 Dodge chassis to build a 750-gpm triple-combination for Clarksville, Tennessee. Credit: Dick Adelman.

Rescue body on a 1961 Dodge cab-forward chassis. Credit: Gerstenslager Corporation.

This is a 1962 Dodge Power Wagon mini pumper with a 250-gpm pump and 300-gallon water tank. It was used in Landsville, New Jersey. Credit: Ray Stevens.

Van Pelt Fire Trucks used this 1966 Dodge chassis to build this high pressure hose wagon for San Mateo, California. Credit: Wayne Sorensen.

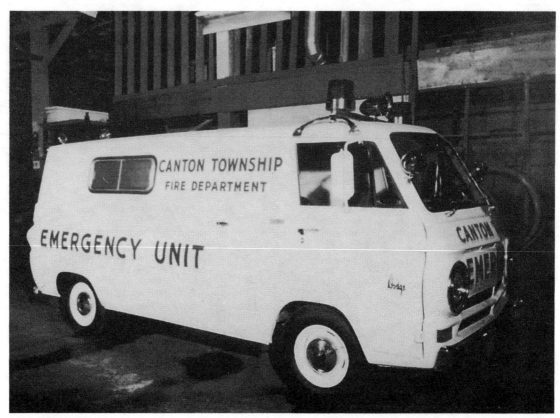

A 1967 Dodge van was used as an emergency unit. Body was outfitted by Gerstenslager. Credit: Gerstenslager Corporation.

Riverton Fire Protection District in Wyoming purchased this Darley 750-gpm triple-combination on a 1961 Ford chassis. Credit: W.S. Darley.

Crown Body & Coach Corporation of Los Angeles used a 1961 Ford C chassis to mount this 65-foot Pitman Snorkel for Carson City, Nevada. Credit: Wayne Sorensen Collection.

1962 Ford Econoline Delivery Van used by the Volunteer Fire Department of Ridgely, Maryland as a rescue and service rig. Credit: Ray Stevens.

A 1963 Ford "N" chassis used by Wynne, Arkansas to build their own 500-gpm triple-combination with a front-mount pump. Credit: Dick Adelman.

A 1964 Ford-Van Pelt 500-gpm combination with a 500-gallon water tank. There is a separate Chrysler engine to run the pump. The short-wheelbase truck was designed for use in the Los Gatos hills. Credit: Wayne Sorensen Collection.

The Bayden, Maryland volunteer fire department purchased this 1965 Ford C tilt cab with a 500-gpm triple-combination from Young Fire Equipment Corporation of Lancaster, New York. Note the windshield at rear. Credit: Ray Stevens.

Jack's Fire Equipment Company built this 500-gpm triple-combination with 1000-gallon water tank for Kuna, Idaho. The rig is mounted on a 1966 Ford chassis with all-wheel-drive. Credit: Wayne Sorensen.

WARD LaFRANCE MODEL: P750-C1000-10

DESIGNED AND BUILT FOR: WEST SAND LAKE
                          FIRE DISTRICT No. 1
                          RENSSELAER COUNTY
                          TOWN OF SAND LAKE, N.Y.

CHIEF: A.S. MILLER   WLF SALESMAN: ED RYSEDORPH

WLF SPEC. No. 7327 OUTLINE DWG: SD-0047 DELIVERED: APRIL 66

ENGINE: FORD 534 V8   PUMP: HALE QLD-75

WHEELBASE: 175"   TANK SIZE: 1000 GALLON

SPECIAL FEATURES: FORD C-1000 CHASSIS - TRANSISTORIZED

IGNITION - POWER STEERING - 110 VOLT 1200 WATT D.C. SYSTEM -

SPECIAL BELL AND SIREN MOUNTING ON CAB - FEDERAL 121A VITALITES

ON REAR STANCHIONS - FEDERAL 14 BEACONS ON CAB - DUAL 12 V

BATTERY SYSTEM - SPECIAL LOCKER AND BODY COMPARTMENTS - HANSEN

LOCKS - 1½" HOSE BED OVER PUMP - ELECTRIC REEL IN REAR.

WARD LAFRANCE TRUCK CORPORATION
ELMIRA HEIGHTS, NEW YORK

This is a catalog sheet reproduced in quantity by Ward LaFrance. It shows a pumper/ tanker rig on a Ford COE chassis that they sold in 1966 to the town of Sand Lake, New York. Ward LaFrance salesmen would distribute this sheet to other likely customers. Credit: Ward LaFrance.

John Bean Division of FMC Corporation used this 1967 Ford F Series chassis to build this triple-combination for Fort Barnwell, North Carolina. Credit: Tony Kelly.

A 1969 Ford with all-wheel-drive, front-mounted pump, and a rear-mounted aerial ladder, outfitted by the Allegheny Fire Equipment Company for the Fort Meyers Beach Fire Control District in Florida. Note pump panels and controls. Credit: Allegheny Fire Equipment Company.

FWD used a 1965 COE chassis for this 750-gpm triple-combination for the Honey Pot Volunteer Hose Company of Nanticoke, Pennsylvania. Ten helmets hang alongside. Credit: Roland Boulet.

Western States Fire Apparatus of Cornelius, Oregon used a 1968 FWD chassis to build a 750-gpm triple-combination with a 1000-gallon booster tank for Tieton, Washington. Notice pump controls are mounted in the front of the cab. Credit: Bill Hattersley.

Western States used a 1969 FWD chassis to build this interesting front-mount pumper for Forest Glen, Oregon. Later, it was sold to the Salsipuedes Fire District near Watsonville, California. Credit: Wayne Sorensen.

This Van Pelt factory photo shows a rig that they built for El Dorado Hills, California, using a 1961 GMC tilt cab chassis. Pump was rated at 1000-gpm. Credit: Van Pelt.

Fire Trucks Incorporated (FTI) of Mount Clemens, Michigan used a 1962 GMC chassis to build a 750-gpm triple-combination for Sand Island, Honolulu, Hawaii. Credit: Dick Adelman.

FTI built this pumper body on a 1960s GMC COE chassis. Credit: FTI.

This 1963 GMC COE was completed by American LaFrance for use as a quint by the Lawrenceburg Fire Department. Credit: Motor Vehicle Manufacturers Association.

Columbia Body & Equipment Company of Portland, Oregon built this 1963 GMC chassis with front-mounted pump for Goshen County, Wyoming. Credit: Columbia Body & Equipment Company.

A 1966 GMC 4000 chassis was used by Van Pelt Fire Trucks to build a triple-combination for Angels Camp, California. Credit: Van Pelt.

Ward LaFrance outfitted this 1970 GMC for the Sheppton-Oneida Volunteer Fire Company. It's a pumper with a large water tank, and it is light-colored. Credit: Ward LaFrance.

During the 1960s, International built a special chassis and front body for use by fire apparatus builders. This chassis was used by Pierce to build a snorkel for Springdale, Arkansas. Close-ups show rear view and pump panel. Credit: Pierce Manufacturing Inc.

The Manhattan Rural Fire District in Montana purchased this 1961 International mounted by Darley with a 750-gpm front-mount pump. Credit: W.S. Darley.

This slip-on unit consists of an independently powered pump, water tank, and hose reel, all on a '60s International flatbed. Credit: W.S. Darley.

An early 1960s International Scout outfitted by Darley with a small slip-on unit was used for plant protection at an International Harvester plant. Credit: W.S. Darley.

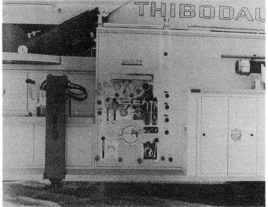

A 1965 International chassis carries a quint body built by Darley for Thibodaux, Louisiana. Close-up shows pump panel and stabilizing jack. Credit: W.S. Darley.

The California Office of Emergency Services places apparatus with fire departments in various communities, which the fire departments may use. In return, the fire department agrees to send the rig, with a crew, when needed elsewhere. This late '60s International Van Pelt is housed with the Woodland, California Fire Department, which has both full-time and volunteer fire fighters. Credit: Don Wood.

A 1968 International with all-wheel-drive, a 750-gpm pump and a 400-gallon booster tank was built by Darley for Rockaway Point, New York, a volunteer unit inside New York City. Credit: W.S. Darley.

A 1968 International tractor, pulling a 6200-gallon tank trailer, was used by the Volunteer Fire Company in Trappe, Maryland. The unit also had a 400-gpm pump. Credit: Ray Stevens.

Kaiser Jeep Corporation used this mid-'60s Kaiser-Jeep Gladiator Series J three-quarter-ton chassis triple-combination fire truck for plant fire protection. Employees served as volunteer plant firemen. Ladders and suction hose are on overhead rack. Credit: Kaiser Jeep Corporation.

The Mack R Model became one of the most popular conventional type trucks in the world. This is Rabbit Creek, Alaska's 1967 Mack R Model 1000-gpm triple-combination with diesel power. Credit: Wayne Sorensen.

This is a tanker with front-mount pump on a 1962 Reo chassis used by Cromwell Valley, New York. Credit: Jim Burner Jr.

Here's another form of volunteer truck. A Utah Power Light and Power truck "volunteered to serve" as a ladder truck on a house fire in Heber City, Utah. Notice that the volunteers are in everyday clothes, not turn-out gear. Credit: John W. Sorensen.

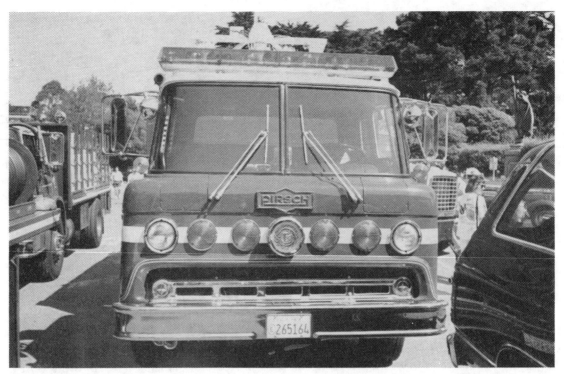

It's sometimes difficult to distinguish between commercial and custom apparatus. This rig, which looks suspiciously like a Ford C series, carries only Pirsch markings. Credit: Don Wood.

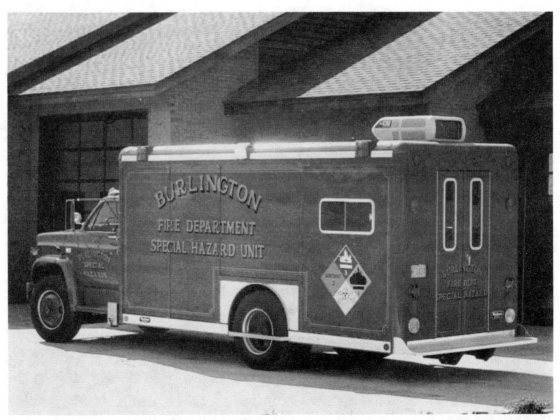

Some fire departments now have special trucks for dealing with hazardous waste spills. Here's a body built by Hackney & Sons Inc. of Washington, North Carolina. Credit: Hackney.

Chapter 8
1971-1980

In the mid-1970s, the Black River Falls, Wisconsin Volunteer Fire Department began operating a county-wide ambulance system. They also switched from relying on a siren to electric pagers. So did Coalinga, California, where one of the benefits was to eliminate the traffic jam caused by non-fire fighters who responded to alarms in order to watch the excitement.

In Iola, Wisconsin, a 100-foot radio tower was erected for use by the Iola Fire Department and the Iola Ambulance Service. In 1976, the Iola department had a total of 10 volunteers who had completed training to become Emergency Medical Technicians. Rollingwood, Texas, a suburb of Austin, had several husband-wife volunteer teams, with the ladies available during the day when the men were working in Austin. "To make sure the women can work Rollingwood's hydrants without having to rely on men, one of the women....regularly checks the 250 or so dotted around the community.' A man may go out with me, but I always screw the caps on the plugs myself. After all, if I can't uncap them, they may as well not be there.'"[1] In 1980 in Terre Hill, Pennsylvania, the volunteer department (all male) "decided that its second engine, a 1957 Chevrolet truck that was converted into a fire engine by a machine shop on the edge of town, should be replaced...." This led to a squabble between the men in the department and their auxiliary (all women), who had decided that they wanted a stronger role in setting policy.[2]

Hazardous spills were becoming a matter of concern. Specialized equipment and training procedures were needed to cope with them. Colored, diamond-shaped placards were carried on trucks and rail cars with symbols that told fire and rescue teams how they should be approached.

To show its continued interest in serving as a chassis supplier to the apparatus outfitting industry, Ford issued a 12-page four-color brochure showing how its various chassis could be used and describing certain features making them adaptable. Such features included "butterfly" hoods with sides that opened upward for rigs requiring front-mount pumps that restrict hood tilting; strategically placed electric junction boxes so additional circuits could be easily added; a set-back front axle option for better maneuverability; and low cab heights to allow for ladders to be carried above.

A significant change in the appearance of apparatus started to take place during this decade. In 1971, a lime yellow fire engine was sold. Studies had shown that the traditional "fire engine red" color was very difficult to see at night in many settings. Ward LaFrance was one of the first apparatus manufacturers to push the sales of the green rigs. According to a statement in 1978 by that company, much of the color research was "provided by Stephen Solomon, an optometrist from nearly Oswego [New York] who has been a volunteer fireman...."[3] Since then, many departments have switched away from the traditional red to lighter colors. This is apparent from pictures in this book.

---

1. House Beautiful (March 1977), page 16.

2. Calvin Trillin, "U.S. Journal: Terre Hill, PA -- The Men and The Women," The New Yorker (Nov. 10, 1980), pages 196-197.

3. Buffalo Courier-Express, Feb. 9 1978, page 20.

Anti-lock brakes became available for heavy trucks, although during the following decade they were the focus of considerable controversy. Other innovations for commercial trucks dealt with improving their energy efficiency. This was because of the dramatic increases in the price of oil and oil products. Fan cutoffs, for example, disengaged the fan when the truck was operating at highway speed and its radiator was being adequately cooled by the stream of air. Streamlining and use of lighter materials also became important. How many of these were factors of importance to fire-fighting rigs is unknown. All departments were paying more for fuel. Strick introduced a very low tractor for tractor-trailer combinations that was so low that it fit below the loaded trailer. Teamsters opposed use of the equipment but the concept shows up in some airport crash trucks and aerial rigs where the cab seems no higher that the roof of a sports car.

Foreign cars had been making inroads into United States markets since the 1960s. By the 1970s, Japanese-built trucks were being marketed on the West Coast, and some European trucks were marketed in the East and Midwest. However, relatively few foreign makes could be found on the rosters of United States fire departments; possibly because of "buy American" policies in municipal purchasing codes.

Some firms rebuild apparatus, and communities may choose to buy a rebuilt custom rig. Here's an excerpt from a current ad from Robeson Fire Trucks, in La Mesa, California, advertising a rebuilt Crown pumper, a make well known in Southern California. Credit: Robeson.

Brockway trucks were built until the mid-1970s. Here's a rescue unit built by Saulsbury on a 1973 Brockway diesel-powered chassis for McLean, New York. Credit: Saulsbury Fire Equipment Corporation.

A 1975 Chevrolet/American LaFrance triple-combination equipped with a 750-gpm pump, 750-gallon water tank and a Detroit 80-71 diesel, built for Gold Flat Fire District, south of Nevada City, California. Credit: Wayne Sorensen.

A 1980 Chevrolet used by the John Bean Division, FMC Corporation, to build a high-pressure squad truck for Heber Valley, Utah. It's shown near a fire; one can see smoke. Credit: John W. Sorensen.

Darley outfitted a plant protection body with a pump on a Cushman chassis. Credit: W.S. Darley.

A '70s Dodge Power Wagon outfitted by Curtis for the Byron Fire District in California.

This is Chestertown, Maryland's 750-gpm front-mounted pump triple-combination on a 1975 Dodge chassis. Credit: Ray Stevens.

Here we see Queenstown, Maryland's 250-gpm mini pumper with a 300-gallon water tank mounted on 1975 Dodge chassis. Credit: Ray Stevens.

Ridgeland, Wisconsin had Darley place the body from an old rig on this 1976 Dodge chassis. Credit: W.S. Darley.

The Salsipuedes Fire Protection District near Watsonville, California used a 1978 Dodge Power Wagon to build this rescue rig. Credit: Wayne Sorensen.

This is East Dover, New Jersey's 1980 Dodge hose tender. It carries 4,000 feet of five-inch hose. Modern hose is much less bulky than that used at mid-century. Credit: Ray Stevens.

Sanford Fire Apparatus Corporation of East Syracuse, New York used this 1980 Dodge Type LCF chassis to build a 1700-gallon tanker with 1000-gpm pump for the Magnolia, Delaware volunteer fire department. Credit: Dick Adelman.

Towers Fire Apparatus Company of Freeburg, Illinois used a Ford C-800 chassis to build a triple-combination for Metropolis, Illinois. It had a Hale pump. Handles on pump controls were to facilitate operation by firefighters wearing gloves. Credit: Towers Fire Apparatus Company.

A mid-'70s Ford F750 was used by Middlesex Fire Equipment Company of Montpelier, Vermont to build a tanker for Johnson, Vermont. The unit carried a 250-gpm portable pump to be used to refill its 1250-gallon tank. At the rear of the tank was a six-inch fast dump, shown dumping the water into an 1100-gallon folding tank that the truck also carried. Credit: David J. Gitchell.

A 1973 Ford-Kidde with a 750-gpm pump and a high expansion foam generator used in Auburn, Washington. Credit: Bill Hattersley.

This is a 1975 Ford C chassis used by Howe Fire Apparatus Company to build this full canopy cab, 1250-gpm triple-combination for Sandy City, Utah. Credit: John F. Sytsma.

A Howe-built quint on a Ford C chassis is powered by a Caterpillar diesel. It has a Waterous pump and a 65-foot rear-mounted aerial ladder. Credit: Howe Fire Apparatus Company.

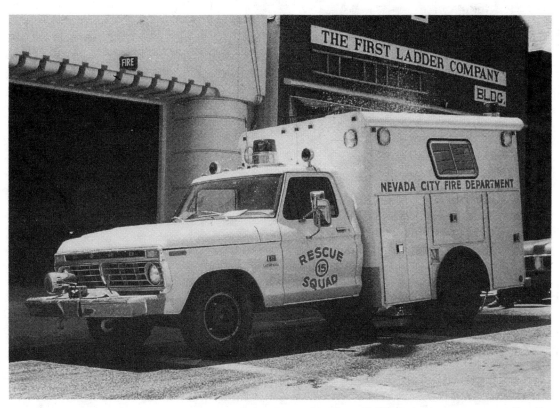

A 1975 Ford F 350 chassis was used for Nevada City, California's rescue car. Credit: Wayne Sorensen.

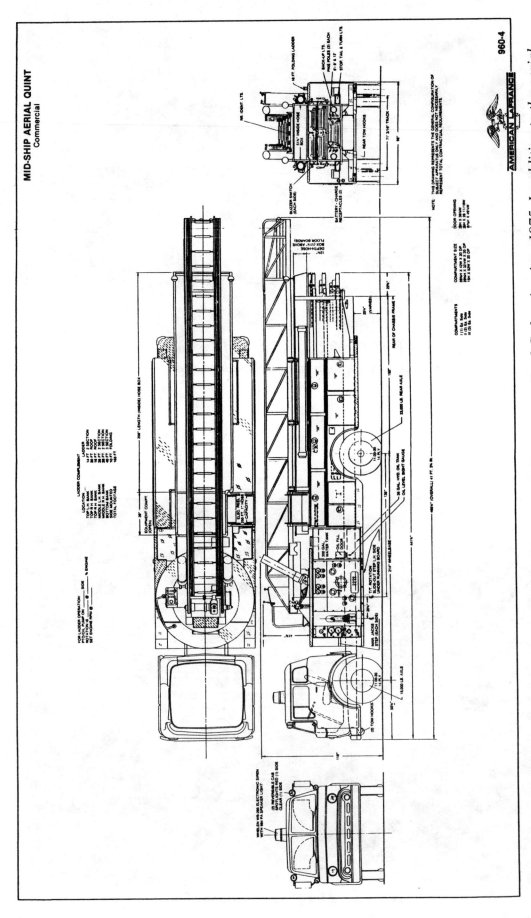

Drawing shows a quint, as would be outfitted by American LaFrance on a Ford C chassis, circa 1975. In addition to the aerial ladder, seven ground ladders are carried. Credit: American LaFrance.

Howe Fire Apparatus Company of Martinez, California used a 1976 Ford L-900 chassis to build this 1700-gallon tanker with a 750-gpm pump for the Salsipuedes Fire Protection District near Watsonville, California. Credit: Wayne Sorensen.

Emergency One built Rapid City, South Dakota's 1250-gpm triple-combination. A 1977 Ford chassis was used. Credit: Wesley Hammond.

A 1979 Ford ambulance is used as a paramedic unit in Campbell, California. Credit: Wayne Sorensen.

The Conroe, Texas volunteer fire department purchased this 1980 Ford 1000-gpm pumper with 1000-gallon booster tank from Pierce Manufacturing Company of Appleton, Wisconsin. Credit: Dave Miller.

A 1980 Ford 900 chassis was used by American LaFrance to build this 1000-gpm quint with a 50-foot Tele-Squint for the Cole-Collister Fire District, near Boise, Idaho. Credit: Wayne Sorensen.

The cover of a full-color 12-page Ford truck brochure issued in 1980 indicates the suitability of a number of their chassis for fire apparatus. Inside there are pictured numerous rigs on four different Ford chassis outfitted by the following firms: A-T-O, Alexis Fire Equipment Corporation, American Fire Apparatus Company, Boardman, Emergency One, General Safety Equipment Corporation, Grumman, National Foam System Inc., Pierce, Saulsbury, and Sutphen. Credit: Ford Heavy Truck Sales.

The Freightliner Corporation of Portland, Oregon built the chassis for Odessa, Maryland's 1979 salvage and rescue rig. Credit: Ray Stevens.

A 1980 GMC Brigadier chassis was used by Van Pelt Fire Trucks of Oakdale, California to build North County Fire District at Castroville, California's 1500-gpm triple-combination with a 900-gallon water tank. The truck was powered by a Detroit 80-71 Diesel. Credit: Wayne Sorensen.

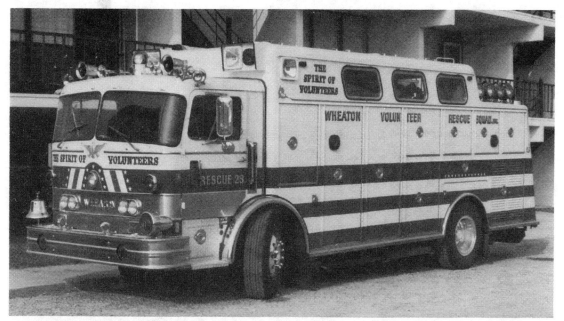

The Providence Body Company of Providence, Rhode Island built this rescue body on a 1971 chassis supplied by Imperial Fire Apparatus Company of Rancocas, New Jersey, for use by the volunteer fire department in Wheaton, Maryland. Credit: Ray Stevens.

The hydraulically powered reel on this rig will hold up to 1200 feet of hose. The chassis is an early '70s International, and the builder was Middlesex Fire Equipment Company. The rig had a 1000-gpm Darley pump and a 500-gallon booster tank. It was used by the volunteer fire department in Washington, Vermont. Credit: David J. Gitchell.

A 1973 International chassis was used by Thibault of Canada to build a 1250-gpm quint with 95-foot snorkel for use in Maple Ridge, British Columbia. Credit: Bill Hattersley.

Here's a 1974 International Fleetstar 2050A with a Howe 750-gpm pump and 900-gallon water tank, powered by a Cat Diesel and built for Morgan Hill Rural Fire District, Morgan Hill California. Credit: Wayne Sorensen.

Watsonville, California used a 1976 International Cargostar 1610 B chassis for its city service truck. Credit: Wayne Sorensen.

The 49er Fire District, near Nevada City, California, had Van Pelt build this 1000-gpm front mount triple-combination on a 1979 International chassis. Credit: Wayne Sorensen.

The Ashland, Virginia Volunteer Fire Department used this 1976 Jeep, which carried 90 gallons of water and had an 80-gpm pump, as a brush rig. Credit: Ray Stevens.

A 1975 Kenworth C-500 chassis carries a Western States Apparatus body that includes a 1250-gpm front-mounted pump and a 2000-gallon tank. The customer was Junction City, Oregon. Credit: Western States Fire Apparatus Inc.

Western States Fire Apparatus of Cornelius, Oregon used a massive 1978 Kenworth chassis with a 1250-gpm front-mounted pump and 2500-gallon water tank for Chelan County Fire District No. 8, Washington. Credit: Western States Fire Apparatus.

The Brumbaugh Body Company of Altoona, Pennsylvania used a 1980 Kenworth chassis to build a 6000-gallon tanker with 1500-gpm pump for Kennett Square, Pennsylvania. Credit: Ray Stevens.

This 1974 Mack CF Series was "top of the line" and had a 1250-gallon pump, 750-gallon water tank, four-door cab, and was built for Pikesville, Maryland. Credit: Ray Stevens.

Cordova, Maryland's Volunteer Firemen's Association uses this 5000-gallon tanker trailer pulled by a 1975 Peterbilt tractor. The rig has a 500-gpm pump, and the hose is carried in coils in racks ahead of the trailer's rear wheels. Credit: Ray Stevens.

Warner-Swasey trucks were built in the period 1955-1977. This Warner-Swasey chassis was used by Van Pelt to build a 1250-gpm triple-combination with a 700-gallon water tank, powered by a Detroit 671 diesel, for Soquel, California. Credit: Wayne Sorensen.

Olean, New York bought this Pierce-outfitted rig carried on a 1980 White chassis and powered by a Detroit diesel. It had a 1250-gpm Waterous pump and a 500-gallon booster tank. Pump controls are on the console, behind the cab, facing rearward. The rig is painted yellow. Credit: Pierce.

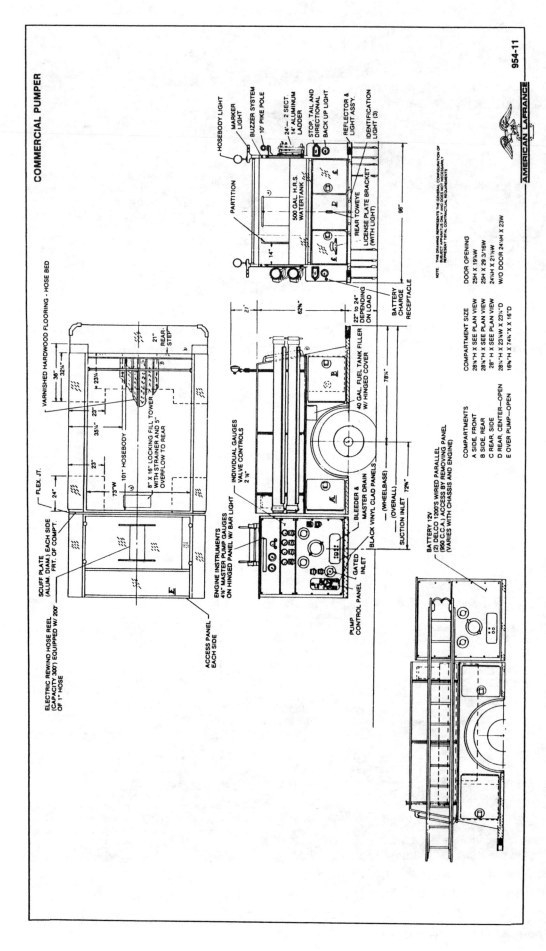

COMMERCIAL PUMPER

954-11

AMERICAN LAFRANCE

Drawings used by American LaFrance in the 1970s show the pumper body that would be placed on any make of commercial chassis. The unit carried a 500-gallon booster tank. Credit: American LaFrance.

Chapter 9
1981-1990

In Corte Madera, California, it was necessary to tear out the entire concrete driveway in front of the fire station and repave it with a much thicker layer of concrete because the weight of the town's fire apparatus had increased to the point that it was breaking the old drive. Fire apparatus were getting larger.

In September 1982, the Pooletown, North Carolina Volunteer Fire Department held their ninth annual Threshers' Reunion and Junior Rodeo, grossing $20,500 and netting more than half of that. "Organizers were disappointed because 102-degree weather on the second day cut the crowd in half of their expectations...."[1] In Nevada City, California, the air horn used to summon volunteers was replaced by a radio alarm system. The department also began using paid drivers to save time getting to fires. Departments expanded their ambulance and emergency medical equipment and personnel. Advances were also made in their ability to deal with hazardous spill incidents.

In Kettering, Ohio, a city of 62,000 people, the fire department was staffed by 40 full-time paid and 100 volunteer fire fighters. In 1984, the city hired a professional "volunteer manager" whose job was "to maintain a viable volunteer fire fighting force to augment the career fire department personnel."[2] This move was taken because of difficulties in sustaining the number of volunteers. The manager's tasks were to recruit new volunteers, retain existing volunteers, and generally increase public recognition of volunteer fire fighters and their importance to Kettering. Families of volunteers were also recognized. On Father's Day, children were given T-shirts with the message: "My Dad's a Kettering Volunteer Fire Fighter." On St. Valentine's Day, coffee mugs that said, "I love a volunteer fire fighter" were given to fire fighters' sweethearts. Campbell, California, which had abandoned volunteers in 1970 in favor of a paid department, began a new program to recruit reserves. To qualify, members had to undergo vigorous training.

In August 1987, St. Paul, Nebraska (north of Grand Island) held a parade. Volunteer departments in neighboring communities sent some entries: Wolbach sent their first rig, a 1927 Chevrolet hose wagon; Cotesfield sent a 1920 chemical cart pulled by an antique auto; and Boelus sent a 1911 American LaFrance pumper that had originally been sold to Omaha and was reputedly one of the earliest motorized fire engines in Nebraska. Early in 1988, Duck Hill, Mississippi (between Jackson and Memphis) took delivery of a C series Ford/Pierce and, in a demonstration for the local press, used the pump connected to the deluge gun to empty the truck's 750-gallon tank is one minute, 21 seconds.[3]

An apparatus industry report in 1983 showed the activities by manufacturer. The largest seven producers in the industry were: American LaFrance, Emergency-One, FMC, Grumman, Mack, Pierce, and Seagrave. The 1983 production of these seven totalled 2196 commercial rigs and 720 custom units. The

1. *The Volunteer Fireman* (fall 1983), page 26.
2. *Public Management* (December 1986), page 26.
3. *Winona* (Mississippi) *Times*, Jan. 21, 1988, page 11.

second group of builders included: 3-D, Darley, Hahn, LTI, P. Thibault, Pierreville, Pirsch, Saulsbury, and Sutphen. The 1983 production of these nine totalled 600 commercial rigs and 252 custom ones. Other manufacturers listed, whose production was believed to be under five units per month each, were: Allegheny, Atlas, Boardman, Continental, Farrar, Fire Appliance, Fire Safety, Fire Tech, Fire X, Four Guys, FTI, Gibson, Indiana Fire, Jim Kirvida, King-Seagrave (Canada), Luverne, Marion Body, Maxim, Middlesex, Quality, Sanford, Smeal, Super-Vac, Superior (Canada), Superior (U.S.), Towers, Ward 79, Westates, Western Fire, and Young. In total, 3780 rigs were tallied, of which 71 percent were on commercial chassis.[4]

The same source also indicated the capacity of the 2801 apparatus pumps shipped in the year 1985: 500-gpm, 12 percent; 750-gpm, 13 percent; 1000-gpm, 29 percent; 1250-gpm, 23 percent; 1500-gpm, 19 percent; 1750-gpm, one percent; and 2000-gpm, three percent.

Another 1985 survey determined that there were 76,625 pumpers and 6910 ladder trucks in use in the United States. The national averages were .318 pumper and .029 ladder truck per 1000 people. In very small communities, the ratio of equipment to people was very high mainly because the number of people was low. An estimate of 1989 sales of new apparatus included 3,846 class A pumpers; 119 mini-pumpers; and 416 aerials.[5]

In the mid-1980s, American LaFrance, once the nation's premier apparatus builder and outfitter, became part of Figgee International Inc. and moved its production to Bluefield, Virginia. Mack dropped out of the custom apparatus market although it continues to supply components used in conjunction with Simox-Duplex chassis. Also, Mack continues to be a popular chassis for other manufacturers to outfit. Several other well-known apparatus manufacturers also closed. In general terms, these operations had been located in the northern United States. Many of the newer firms were in the South. Other firms either entered or left the market, sometimes with the new one taking over the space vacated by another. Kovatch Mobile Equipment (KME) marketed much of its line on Navistar chassis.

Allowable widths for trucks on the highway was increased to 102 inches, which was eventually reflected in the width of all large trucks. Several foreign truck manufacturers entered into marketing and manufacturing agreements with U.S. truck builders.

This picture appeared in literature from the Reading Body Company in the mid-1970s, showing an open rescue body mounted on a commercial chassis. Credit: Reading Body Works Inc.

---

4. *Information courtesy of the Fire Apparatus Manufacturers Association.*
5. *Information courtesy of the Fire Apparatus Manufacturers Association.*

A 1985 Chevrolet-Kodiak chassis was used by Grumman to build a 1000-gpm triple-combination for Everson, Washington. It also carried a 750-gallon water tank. Credit: Bill Hattersley.

This is a 1986 Chevrolet C-34 pickup converted into brush truck 29-0 by the Port Penn, Maryland Volunteer Fire Company. This truck has four-wheel-drive with all-terrain tires. This pumper unit provides rapid initial action on incipient fires. It transports a crew of three men, approximately 1,000 pounds of auxiliary equipment and tools, 200 gallons of water, and pumping equipment. Notice the roll bars. Credit: Ray Stevens.

The Star Cross Volunteer Fire Company of Franklin Township, New Jersey purchased this 1990 Dodge/Pierce mini pumper. Credit: Ray Stevens.

The Boys Town Volunteer Fire Department in Nebraska uses this 1983 Ford/Pierce with a 1000-gpm pump and a 750-gallon tank. Credit: Pierce.

Westates Truck Equipment Corporation of Menlo Park, California used a 1983 Ford C chassis with tilt cab to build this 1000-gpm pumper for Branciforte, California. Credit: Wayne Sorensen.

Oxford, Pennsylvania's triple-combination is mounted on a 1983 Ford C chassis by Pierce. Note the big hose reel in the rear of the truck for a six-inch hose. Credit: Roland Boulet.

Underwriters Labs tests all pumps. Dixon, Kentucky bought this Darley-outfitted Ford with a 750-gpm pump in 1984. The document dated Sept. 13, 1984 is the builder's record of pump construction, and the document dated a day later is the Underwriters' test results. Credit: W.S. Darley.

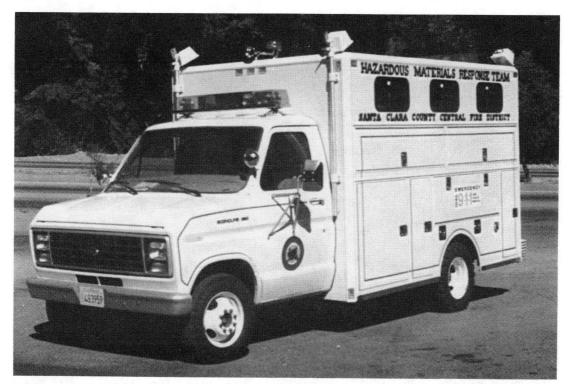

Here is a 1985 Ford Econoline 350 Hazardous Materials Response Team's apparatus in service in the Santa Clara County (California) Central Fire District. Credit: Wayne Sorensen.

Van Pelt-FMC of Oakdale, California built this 1000-gpm triple-combination on a 1986 Ford F-800 chassis with a Detroit diesel for the 49er Fire District near Nevada City, California. Credit: Wayne Sorensen.

Towers Fire Apparatus of Freeburg, Illinois built this rig for use in Sparta, Illinois on a 1988 Ford L8000 chassis. It has a 1000-gpm pump, a 500-gallon booster tank, and a rear-mounted 55-foot ladder. Credit: Towers.

A 1988 Ford F-350 Super Cab pickup with slip-on 150-gpm pump and 150-gallon tank unit was used by the Volunteer Firemen's Association of Cordova, Maryland as a brush truck. Credit: Ray Stevens.

"Attack" pumpers became popular during the 1980s. They were smaller and designed for a small crew to reach the fire scene more quickly. Often it was intended that they were to be followed by a larger, more heavily manned piece of apparatus. This 1990 Ford F-350 was outfitted by Saulsbury for the volunteer fire company in Shinglehouse, Pennsylvania. It has a 750-gpm Hale pump. Credit: Saulsbury Fire Equipment Corporation.

A 1989 Freightliner chassis was used by Anderson Engineering of Langley, British Columbia to build a 1750-gpm triple-combination for Delta, British Columbia. Note roll-up equipment doors. Credit: Bill Hattersley.

Emergency One used a 1981 GMC 4X4 chassis to build Eagle Nest, New Mexico's 750-gpm pumper with a top-mounted console. It had an all-wheel-drive chassis. Pump controls were in a console that the operator would reach by climbing behind the cab. Credit: Emergency One.

Pierce Manufacturing Company of Appleton, Wisconsin used a 1981 GMC all-wheel-drive chassis to mount Laury's Station, Arizona's pumper. Because of the rig's increased height, original headlights replaced with red lights and new headlights are mounted just above bumper. Credit: Dick Adelman.

The Welch Fire Equipment Company of Marion, Wisconsin used a 1982 GMC to build a 750-gpm triple-combination for Caldwell, Idaho. Credit: Wayne Sorensen Collection.

American LaFrance used this 1984 GMC-Commodore chassis to mount this 1000-gpm pump and 1000-gallon water tank triple-combination rig for Madison County, Idaho. Credit: American LaFrance.

FMC-Van Pelt used a 1985 GMC chassis to build a 1000-gpm triple-combination for Felton, California. Credit: Wayne Sorensen.

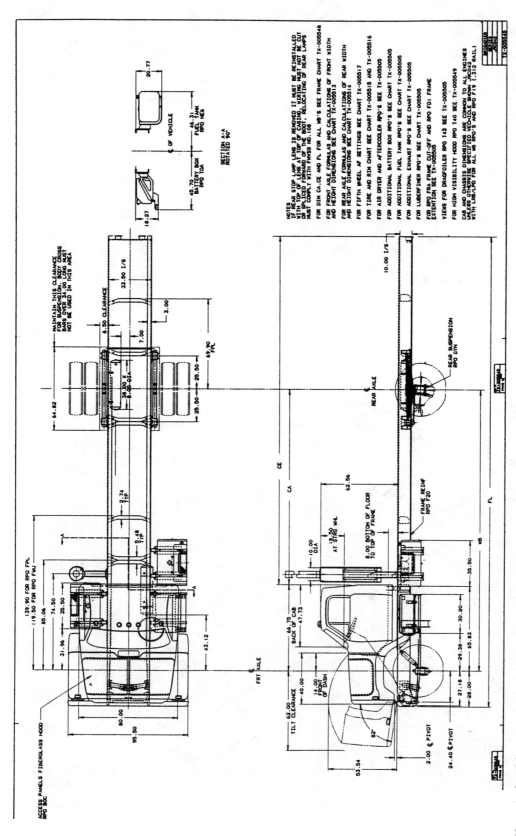

Chassis builders provide books of engineering drawings showing the dimensions of their various chassis. Apparatus outfitters then adapt their bodies to fit the chassis. These drawings are for a 1985 GMC Brigadier. Not shown are the rear and front views. Most of the notes in the lower right corner refer to charts or additional, more detailed drawings. Credit: GMC Truck & Coach.

A 1986 GMC 4X4 Jimmy chief's car of the 49er Fire District near Nevada City, California. Credit: Wayne Sorensen.

The FMC Corporation used a 1990 GMC Brigadier chassis to build this 1250-gpm triple-combination for Bonneville Fire Protection District No. 1 in Idaho Falls, Idaho. Credit: Wayne Sorensen.

Emergency One used a 1981 Hendrickson all-wheel-drive chassis for Whittier, Alaska's 1500-gpm triple-combination with 1000-gallon water tank. Credit: Emergency One.

Pierce built this rig for Harvard, Illinois on a 1981 International chassis. It carries a 1000-gpm Waterous pump, a 400-gallon booster tank, and a 55-foot LTI "Firestick" aerial device. Credit: Pierce.

A 1982 International COE Cargostar chassis was used by Anderson Engineering of Langley, British Columbia, to build Whistler, British Columbia a 1250-gpm quint with a 55-foot "Firestick." Credit: Bill Hattersley.

An early '80s International on an all-wheel-drive chassis was outfitted by FTI. Note the pump control panel to the right of the front-mounted pump. Credit: FTI.

Task Master Equipment Company of Dundee, Illinois used a 1984 Kenworth chassis to build a 3000-gallon tanker with a 1250-gpm pump for Cape May Court House, Middle Township, Maryland. Credit: Ray Stevens.

Van Pelt Fire Truck, FMC of Oakdale, California used a 1985 Kenworth COE chassis to build this 1500-gpm triple-combination for the Aptos-La Selva Fire District, Aptos, California. Credit: Wayne Sorensen.

Brown Deer, Wisconsin uses this 1981 Mack with a crew cab. It was built by Pierce and has a 1500-gpm Waterous pump and a 500-gallon booster tank. Credit: Pierce.

A 1984 Nissan pickup is used as a utility truck by the 49er Fire District near Nevada City, California. Credit: Wayne Sorensen.

A 1988 Peterbilt chassis is used for fire and rescue Squad No. 6 of the Volunteer Fire Department of Huntingtown, Maryland. Credit: Ray Stevens.

Emergency One mounted the rescue squad for Byron, Illinois on a 1981 Spartan chassis. Credit: Emergency One.

The Salsipuedes Fire District near Watsonville, California purchased this 1250-gpm pumper on a 1985 Spartan chassis from Western States Fire Apparatus of Cornelius, Oregon. Credit: Wayne Sorensen.

A 1984 Volvo N10 chassis was used by Van Pelt to build a 2500-gallon tank with a 1000-gpm pump for West Valley, Washington. Credit: Bill Hattersley.

A few manufacturers build chassis for other apparatus manufacturers to complete. Because fire fighters can no longer hang onto the outside of a rig and because of the bulky breathing apparatus they now carry, most conventional truck cabs are too small. Shown here is a cab and chassis built by Spartan Motors of Charlotte, Michigan for other outfitters to complete. The picture of the open door shows a Spartan rig built for FMC to complete; the FMC emblem is embossed in the upholstery. Credit: Spartan.

Mounting an assembled firefighting body onto a chassis, using a form of forklift truck. Note that the pump has already been installed midship on the chassis. Credit: Emergency One Inc.

Chapter 10
1991-1992

Traffic Safety magazine, in its March/April 1991 issue, described the 20-year campaign of Dr. Stephen Solomon, the Oswego, New York optometrist and volunteer fire fighter mentioned earlier, to have fire apparatus painted lime yellow. According to the article, prior to 1970, about 85 percent of new apparatus were painted red; in 1990, 40 percent were painted lime yellow. The majority of new apparatus are still red for two reasons, both related to tradition: departments like the color because it is traditional, and motorists associate the red color with fire apparatus.

An article in the June 1992 *Reader's Digest* describing the service of a volunteer emergency medical technician (EMT) in Lake of the Woods, Virginia, contained this sentence about the department's equipment:

"The Lake of the Woods volunteer rescue squad started out with a used ambulance and a first-aid box. Now, 18 years later, it operates with two fully equipped Advanced Life Support units, one Shock Trauma unit and a crash truck."[1]

By 1991, the Santa Clara County Central Fire Protection District, which consists of a number of departments whose beginnings were described earlier, now was responsible for protecting a population of 125,000 covering 100 square miles. There were a total of nine fire stations, 155 paid firemen and 75 volunteers. These volunteers still assist paid personnel, and the volunteers are called by pagers and radio. During the fire season, tankers are stationed at various areas throughout in order for the volunteers to make a quick response. The district provides fire protection to the cities of Cupertino, Los Gatos, Saratoga, Monte Sereno and numerous unincorporated areas.

Fire safety is a big concern for the district, and it joined with the San Jose Water Works in September 1992 in setting the stage for a new confrontation with the city of Monte Sereno over fire safety in the West Valley foothills. The battle has flared for months about dangerously "inadequate" fire-fighting water supplies in the foothills. At issue is Monte Sereno's reluctance to demand that expensive interior sprinkler systems or new outside fire hydrants be installed when hillside homes are remodeled or enlarged. During the past year, the Monte Sereno City Council has granted a number of homeowners exemptions from fire-district sprinkler and hydrant requirements. In August 1992, the fire district reiterated its commitment to sprinklers and hydrants because "the possibility of an Oakland Hills-type fire occurring in the Monte Sereno areas exists primarily due to the similar weather conditions, vegetation and terrain." The district has resisted efforts by Monte Sereno to "reduce the minimum fire-flow of water for dwelling structures to a lesser volume" than the 1000 gallons a minute required in the 1991 Uniform Fire Code. Developers must meet current standards that have been developed from lessons learned from natural disasters, such as the 1989 Loma Prieta earthquake, the 1990 freeze and the 1991 Oakland Hills fire.

---

*1. Pat Ivey, "Rescue Squad!" **Reader's Digest** (June 1992), page 164.*

In Iola, Wisconsin, the volunteer fire department celebrated its centennial in 1992 by publishing a history. The booklet's closing words were:

"Volunteers! What would we do without them? They fight and extinguish many fires and help prevent others. They rush to aid the sick and injured and have saved lives. It is easy to take them for granted, but they are always there when we need them."

In recent years, the quality of service in response to medical emergencies has improved along with an increase in geographic areas of coverage. Volunteer fire departments deserve much of the credit. Today, many of them run ambulances or paramedic vehicles. Here, in Maupin, Oregon we see an ambulance on a Ford chassis housed next to a Maxim fire engine. Credit: Don Wood.

An early '90s FWD chassis carries an "Aerialscope" marketed by Baker Equipment Engineering Company. The Aerialscope is a 95-foot telescoping crane carrying a fire-fighting platform that was originally developed for use with Mack apparatus. However, in 1990, Mack discontinued manufacture of the appropriate chassis. Credit: Baker.

A 1991 GMC chassis was used by Central Fire Truck Corporation to build a 1250-gpm pumper with a 750-gallon water tank for Asotin, Washington. Credit: Bill Hattersley.

The Rural-Metro Fire Department in Knox County, Tennessee uses this 1991 International Emergency One 1250-gpm pumper with a 1500-gallon water tank. Credit: Dick Adelman.

A 1991 International tanker built by Hi-Tech Fire Apparatus of Oakdale, California is owned and operated by some former Van Pelt fire truck employees. Credit: Hi-Tech.

Folsum, Pennsylvania purchased this 1991 International 1000-gpm triple-combination built by Kovatch Mobile Equipment Corporation. Credit: KME.

A 1991 Mack chassis was outfitted by 3D of Shawano, Wisconsin for the Ephraim, Wisconsin fire department. The rig carries a 1500-gpm Hale pump and a steel 1000-gallon booster tank. Credit: 3D.

The New Pittsburg Volunteer Fire Department in Wooster, Ohio purchased this 1991 Mack that had been outfitted by 3D with a 1250-gpm Hale pump and a 1000-gallon booster tank. Credit: 3D.

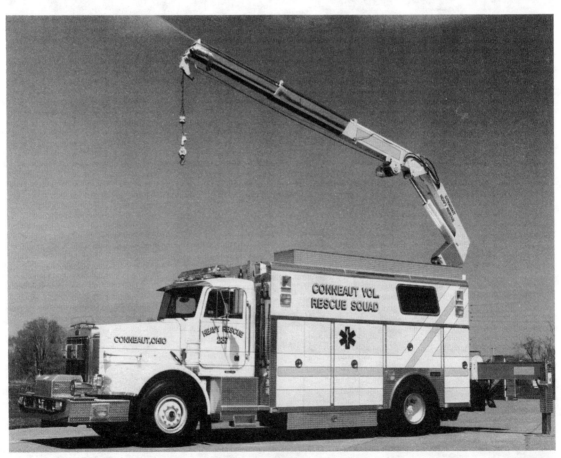

Conneaut, Ohio's volunteer rescue squad uses this 1990s Peterbilt rescue squad built for them by Saulsbury Fire Equipment Corporation of Tully, New York. The crane has a 19,000-pound capacity and is designed for use in trench rescue, vehicle stabilization, etc. In addition, it can be used to launch the squad's airboat by placing it in the water next to one of the city's many bridges. Credit: Saulsbury.

The Denton Volunteer Fire Company in Caroline County, Maryland runs this 1991 White-GMC rig that carries a 3500-gallon tank and a 1500-gpm front-mounted pump. Credit: Ray Stevens.

Components used in outfitting apparatus also change. This is is a contemporary warning light system. The angular design is to increase its effectiveness at street intersections. Credit: Federal Signal Corporation.

Bibliography

"Asheville Fire Ladies Protect Community," *The American City* (June 1946), p. 7.

Birchfield, Rodger, *New Stutz Fire Apparatus Company* (Hartford City, IN: Birchfield, 1980).

Boucher, David, *Ride the Devil Wind* (Bellflower, CA: Fire Publications Inc., 1991).

"Business End of a Volunteer Fire Department," *The American City* (February 1951), p. 122.

Carpadus, Norman and Kitty, *The Petaluma Fire Department 1857 to 1964* (Petaluma, CA: Fire Department, 1963).

Chiles, James R., "It's Not Easy Going Eye to Eye With Today's Newfangled Fires," *Smithsonian* (May 1992), pp. 32-41.

"Citizen-Firemen," *The New York Times Magazine* (Dec. 23, 1941), p. 13.

Community Forest Fire Fighting Equipment (Boston: National Fire Protection Association, 1934).

Conway, W. Fred, *Chemical Fire Engines* (New Albany, IN: Fire Buff House, 1987).

Crismon, Fred W., *U.S. Military Wheeled Vehicles* (Sarasota, FL: Crestline, 1983).

Daly, George Anne & Robrecht, John J., *An Illustrated Handbook of Fire Apparatus with Emphasis on 19th Century American Pieces* (Philadelphia: INA Corporation Archives Department, 1972).

Daniel, James, "How Good Are Our Volunteer Firemen?" *Reader's Digest* (June 1968), pp. 118-122.

Eckart, Harvey, *Mack Fire Apparatus, A Pictorial History* (Middletown, NY: The Engine House, 1990).

Fire Apparatus Photo Album of the Greenfield Village Musters (Naperville, IL: The Visiting Fireman, 1984).

Fire Apparatus Photo Album of the Valhalla Musters (Naperville, IL: The Visiting Fireman, 1983).

"Fire Company Members Help Buy Equipment," *The American City* (July 1927), pp. 89-90.

"Fire Station for Volunteers Designed for Easy Adaptation to Paid Department," *The American City* (April 1928), pp. 131-132.

"Fireman, Save Me--As A Hobby," *Nation's Business* (October 1948), pp. 36-38, 66-68.

Frady, Steven R., *Red Shirts and Leather Helmets, Volunteer Fire Fighting on the Comstock Lode* (Reno: University of Nevada Press, 1984).

Frederickson, Fred R., *Oil But No Water--A History of The Coalinga Fire Department* (Coalinga, CA: Fire Department, 1980).

"Glimpses into a Village Fire Department," *The American City* (September 1960), p. 126.

Gnacinski, Janneyne L, compiler, *Iola Fire Department Centennial* (Iola, WI: The Iola Historical Society, 1992).

Graham, James S., *Mountain View and The Men Who Protect It From Fire* (Mountain View, CA: City of Mountain View, 1963).

"Growth of a Small Town Fire Department," *The American City* (March 1958), p. 26.

Hagy, Steve, *Howe Fire Apparatus Album* (Naperville, IL: The Visiting Fireman, 1984).

Hart, Arthur A., *Fighting Fires on the Frontier* (Boise, ID: Boise Fire Department Association, 1976).

Hubert, Philip G., Jr., "Fire-fighting today and tomorrow," *Scribners* (October 1902), pp. 449-466.

Malecky, John M., *Mack Tilt Cab Fire Apparatus* (Staten Island, NY: Fire Apparatus Journal Publications, 1988).

Margolis, Richard J. "For Volunteers, Dousing Flames Is Only Part of the Job," *Smithsonian* (November 1983), pp. 154-163.

McCall, Walter, *American Fire Engines Since 1900* (Glen Ellyn, IL: Crestline, 1976).

McCosker, M. J., *The Historical Collection of Insurance Company of North America* (Philadelphia: I.N.A., 1967).

Metcalf, Woodbridge, "Tank Trucks for Rural and Forest Fire Fighting," *Journal of Forestry* (May 1933), pp. 522-532.

"Methods of Financing Volunteer Fire Departments," *The American City* (May 1929), pp. 542-543.

"Methods of Pay and Training for Part-Paid Fire Departments," *The American City* (November 1929), p. 21.

William, Myrna, *Chico Fire Department* (Chico, CA: Printing & Publishing Company, 1973).

National Fire Protection Association, *Community Equipment and Organization for Fighting Forest, Grass, and Brush Fires* (Boston: The Association, 1956).

"Neighborhood Civilian Fire Departments," *The American City* (May 1942), p. 56.

Redford, L. B., "The Volunteer Fire Department and Its Problems," *The American City* (October 1922), pp. 344-345.

Reichhardt, George C., ed., *Darley Fire Apparatus Photo Album* (Naperville, IL: The Visiting Fireman, 1987).

Sorensen, Lorin, *The Commercial Fords* (St. Helena, CA: Silverado Publishing Company, 1984).

Sorensen, Wayne and Donald F. Wood, *Motorized Fire Apparatus of the West 1900-1960* (Polo, IL: Transportation Trails, 1991).

Stroh, J.W., "Maintaining the Efficiency of a Volunteer Fire Department," *The American City* (January 1923), pp. 36-37.

Tisdale, Sally, "Bound Upon a Wheel of Fire," *Harper's Magazine* (January 1990), pp. 76-77.

Trillin, Calvin, "U.S. Journal: Terre Hill, PA., The Men and The Women," *The New Yorker* (Nov. 10, 1980), pp. 192-200.

Troyer, Howard William, *The Four Wheel Drive Story* (New York: McGraw-Hill, 1954).

Wade, Herbert T., "Automobile Fire Engines," *Scientific American* (Jan. 15, 1910), pp. 54-55, 69-70.

Wagner, James K, *Ford Trucks Since 1905* (Glen Ellyn, IL: Crestline, 1978).

"Well-fixed Team of Fire Eaters," *Life* (April 25, 1960), p. 65.

White, Bailey, "I'm all suited up and a fireman for life," *Smithsonian* (November 1990), p. 206.

Winchester, James H., "Volunteer Firemen: Heroes Without Pay," *Popular Science* (May 1969), pp. 94-97; 206.

Wood, Donald F., "All Fired Up," *Special-Interest Autos* (April 1981), pp. 54-60.

----------, "Trucks at Work: Fire Engines," *Wheels of Time* (April 1981), pp. 13-15.

Wren, James A. and Genevieve J., *Motor Trucks of America* (Ann Arbor: The University of Michigan Press, 1979).

"Yes, We Now Have Firewomen," *House Beautiful* (March 1977), pp. 12-20.

Manufacturers Index

A

A.L. Hansen Manufacturing Company 208
Abbott-Downing Truck and Body Company 69
Adam Black Body Company 91
Ahrens-Fox 104, 146, 156, 209, 231
Ahrens-Fox Fire Engine Company 196
Alexis Fire Equipment Corporation 291
Allegheny Fire Equipment Company 263
American Fire Apparatus 220, 221, 291
American LaFrance 36, 40, 41, 59, 60, 61, 62, 64,
        65, 77, 80, 81, 84, 95, 100, 124, 127,
        144, 164, 187, 214, 219, 232, 233, 234,
        235, 267, 288, 291, 300, 312
Anderson Engineering 310, 316
Apparatus Outfitters 82
Approval Fire Equipment Company 203, 224
Approved Fire Apparatus 238
Approved Fire Equipment Company 209
Attack 309
Atterbury 36
Auto Car Equipment Company 27
Autocar 164, 210, 211
Available Truck Company 211

B

Baker Equipment Engineering Company 325
Barton 123, 137, 143, 151, 165, 195, 221
Bickle Fire Engines Ltd. 84
Boardman 172, 188, 291
Boyer 68, 74, 82, 98, 210
Brockway 60, 61, 62, 279
Brumbaugh Body Company 229, 297
Buffalo Fire Apparatus 89, 90,. 105, 106, 122, 153
Buick 116

C

C.D. Beck 209, 231
Cadillac 62, 63
Caterpillar 287, 294
Central Fire Truck Corporation 171, 219, 224, 325
Chadwick Great Six 37
Challenger 126, 174
Champion 85, 210
Chas. T. Holloway & Company 17
Chevrolet 63, 64, 65, 66, 67, 68, 116, 117, 118,
        119, 120, 157, 158, 165, 166, 167, 168,
        169, 170, 171, 172, 173, 209, 212, 213,
        214, 251, 252, 253, 254, 255, 279, 280,
        303
Chrysler 260
Chrysler Airstream 124

Coast 175, 232, 235, 239, 243
Columbia Body & Equipment Company 267
Commerce 68
Concord 69
Continental 95
Corbitt 69, 173, 214, 215
Cosmopolitan 61, 62
Cowing 17, 21
Crown 278
Crown Body & Coach Corporation 259
Curtis 281
Curtis-Heiser 145
Cushman 280

D

Darley 60, 66, 67, 113, 130, 160, 161, 169, 178,
        185, 190, 205, 226, 234, 240, 247, 258,
        270, 271, 273, 280, 282, 293, 306
Dart Motor Truck Company 38
Day Elder Motor Truck Company 70
DeSoto Airflow 124
Detroit 279, 292, 299, 307
Diamond T 120, 121, 122, 174, 175, 215, 248, 255
DiMartini 70
Dodge 38, 72, 84, 123, 124, 125, 176, 177, 178,
        179, 180, 182, 216, 217, 218, 219, 256,
        257, 258, 281, 282, 283, 284, 304
Dorris Motor Car Company 73
Duplex 219

E

E.H. Stokes Fire Company 91
Eagle Hose Company 109
Eaton Metal Products 134
Emergency One 289, 291, 310, 315, 319, 326
Empire Engine Company of San Jose 15

F

FABCO 177
Fageol 73, 126
Federal 39, 74, 181, 220
Fire Trucks Incorporated 266
FMC 263, 280, 312, 314, 317, 321
Foamite-Childs Corporation 88
Ford 39, 40, 41, 42, 66, 75, 76, 77, 78, 126, 127,
        128, 129, 130, 131, 132, 133, 134, 135,
        136, 137, 180, 184, 185, 186, 187, 188,
        220, 221, 222, 223, 224, 225, 226, 258,
        259, 260, 261, 262, 263, 276, 284, 285,
        286, 287, 288, 289, 290, 291, 304, 305,
        306, 307, 308, 309, 324

Franklin 42
Freightliner 292, 310
FTI 316
FWD 43, 78, 79, 138, 139, 189, 226, 227, 228, 264,
        265, 325

G

Garford Motor Truck Company 44
General Body Company 208
General Fire Truck Corporation 140, 141
General Manufacturing Company 77
General Monarch 140
General Safety Equipment Corporation 291
Gerstenslager 251, 254, 258
Gleason & Bailey 16
GMC 79, 80, 81, 139, 141, 190, 229, 230, 231, 232,
        233, 265, 266, 267, 268, 292, 310, 311,
        312, 313, 314, 325
Goodwill Fire Company 48
Gotfredson Truck Corporation 84
Graham Brothers 81, 82, 83, 84
Gramm Bernstein 45
Grass-Premier 85
Gray Fire Apparatus 241
Grumman 291, 303

H

Hackney & Sons Inc. 276
Hale 101, 109, 145, 193, 211, 222, 284, 309, 327,
        328
Haney 253
Heil Tank 164
Heiser Body Company 218
Hendrickson 315
Hercules 145, 149
Hi-Tech Fire Apparatus 326
Holloway 27
Holloway Chemical Engine 19
Howard-Cooper 118
Howe 26, 64, 129, 149, 195, 225, 240, 286, 287,
        289, 294
Hudson 85

I

Imperial Fire Apparatus Company 293
Indiana 141, 142
Indiana-Van Pelt 142
International 28, 44, 46, 86, 143, 144, 191, 192,
        193, 194, 234, 235, 236, 239, 248, 269,
        270, 271, 272, 273, 293, 294, 295, 315,
        316, 326, 327

International Motor Company 52

J

Jack's Fire Equipment Company 261
Jeep 240, 296
Jeffers Company 16

K

K-5 73
Kaiser Jeep Corporation 274
Kearns-Dughie 88
Kenworth 145, 196, 241, 296, 297, 317
Kissel 47
Knox 29, 47, 48
Kovatch Mobile Equipment Corporation 327

L

L.N. Curtis & Sons 218, 233
Larrabee 89
Larrabee-Deyo Motor Truck Company 89
LCF 284
LeBlond-Schacht 146, 196
Lincoln 90, 91
Locomobile 48
Luverne 148, 213

M

Maccar 91
Mack 49, 91, 92, 93, 147, 148, 197, 209, 242, 274, 298, 318, 325, 327, 328
Marmon 93
Marmon-Herrington 220
Maxim 324
Maxim Motor Company 126, 222
Maxwell-Briscoe Motor Company 50, 94
Mercedes 28
Middlesex Fire Equipment Company 285, 293
Morelands 94

N

Nash 95
National Foam System Inc. 291
Nelson Equipment Company 212
New Stutz Fire Apparatus Company 142
Nissan 318
Northern 95
Northern Fire Apparatus Company 44
Nott 28, 95
Nott-Universal 96

O

O.J. Childs Company 80
Obenchain-Boyer Company 103, 155
Oren-Roanoke 167, 173, 184, 186, 211, 214, 215, 223, 243
Oshkosh 97, 149

P

Pacific Fire Extinguisher Company 133
Packard 96, 149, 150
Paramount 98
Peter Pirsch and Sons 56, 70, 121
Peterbilt 243, 298, 328
Pierce 54, 228, 269, 290, 291, 299, 305, 311, 315, 318
Pierce-Arrow 98
Pirsch 51, 96, 97, 108, 112, 131, 138, 146, 158, 159, 174, 198, 276
Pitman Snorkel 259
Pope Manufacturing Company 29
Pope-Hartford 30
Procter Keefe Body Company 205
Prospect Fire Engine Company 78
Providence Body Company 293

Q

QMC 157, 168

R

Reading Body Company 302
Redwine Company 39
Reo 51, 66, 99, 100, 101, 151, 152, 153, 198, 244, 275
Robeson Custom Fire Trucks 222
Robeson Fire Trucks 278
Robinson Fire Apparatus Manufacturing Company 37
Rumsey and Company 18

S

Sanford 102, 103
Sanford Fire Apparatus Corporation 154
Sanford Motor Truck Company 102
Sauer 52
Saulsbury 279, 291, 309
Schacht 104, 146
Schnabel Company 248
Schneer 53
Seagrave 19, 117, 118, 129, 132, 135, 136, 152, 165, 175, 183, 256
Seddon 105
Seddon Bros. 105
Selden 105
Service Motor Truck Company 53
Silsby 18
Sims Fire Equipment Company 101
Spartan 319, 320, 321
Star Compound Six 106
Stewart 106, 153, 154
Stoughton Wagon Company 107
Studebaker 108, 155, 156, 198
Stutz 141, 158
Stutz Fire Engine Company 142
Sutphen 291

T

Task Master Equipment Company 193, 317
Thibault 294
Thomas 54
Towers Fire Apparatus Company 284, 308
Transport Truck Company 108

U

U.S. Fire Apparatus 119

V

Van Pelt 144, 176, 193, 199, 203, 204, 215, 245, 257, 265, 268, 272, 292, 295, 299, 307, 317, 320, 326
Viking 126
Volvo 320

W

W.S. Darley & Company 136
W.S. Nott Company 101
W.S. Nott Fire Engine Company 112
Walter 30, 157
Ward LaFrance 122, 125, 134, 180, 199, 252, 262, 268
Warner-Swasey 299
Waterous 26, 31, 46, 54, 287, 299, 315, 318
Waterous Engine Works 75
Webb Motor Fire Apparatus Company 54
Welch Fire Equipment Company 311
Wesco Fire Division 255
Westates Truck Equipment Corporation 305
Western States Fire Apparatus 296, 297, 320
Westinghouse Gasoline Fire Engine 23
White 32, 55, 56, 109, 110, 111, 158, 159, 176, 199, 200, 201, 202, 203, 204, 243, 245, 246, 247, 299, 329
Willys-Overland 112
Winther Motor Truck Company 56
Winton 112

Location Index

A

Alaska
    Nome, 118
    Rabbit Creek, 190, 274
    Sand Lake, 180
    Whittier, 315
Arizona
    Laury's Station, 311
    Winslow, 183
Arkansas
    Bentonville, 188
    Jonesboro, 222
    Springdale, 269
    West Memphis, 135
    Wynne, 260

B

British Columbia
    Delta, 310
    Langley, 310, 316
    Maple Ridge, 253, 294
    Whistler, 316

C

California 94, 216, 281
    Alameda, 31
    Amaden, 20
    Angels Camp, 268
    Aptos, 317
    Atascadero, 176, 193
    Belmont, 73
    Ben Lomond, 204
    Berkeley, 42
    Bonny Doon, 93
    Boulder Creek, 81, 233
    Branciforte, 243
    Bryte, 245
    Cambria, 123
    Campbell, 40, 142, 290
    Capitola, 242
    Castroville, 292
    El Dorado Hills, 265
    Felton, 312
    Hayward, 230
    Healdsburg, 40
    La Mesa, 222, 278
    Lake Grove, 185
    Live Oak, 232
    Livermore, 197
    Los Angeles, 76, 133, 239, 259
    Los Gatos, 246, 260

Martinez, 239, 243, 289
Marysville, 18
Menlo Park, 104, 305
Milbrae, 174
Mill Valley, 70
Monterey County, 199
Morgan Hill, 218, 294
Mountain View, 39
Nevada City, 14, 52, 226, 279, 287, 295, 307, 314, 318
Oakdale, 176, 292, 307, 317, 326
Oakland, 133, 218
Pacifica, 212
Pasadena, 93
Redwood City, 53
Sacramento, 126, 174
Salida, 147
Salinas, 144
Samoa, 246
San Carlos, 125, 199
San Francisco, 53, 201
San Jose, 230
San Mateo, 257
Santa Clara County, 215, 229, 239, 307
Santa Clara, 42, 221
Santa Cruz, 201
Santa Fe Spring, 111
Scotts Valley, 164
Soquel, 299
Sunnyvale, 255
Union City, 203
Valley of the Moon, 41
Walnut Creek, 116
Watsonville, 265, 283, 289, 295, 320
Winters, 126
Woodland, 83, 272
Woodside, 147
Colorado
    Gold Hill, 134
    Golden, 190
Connecticut
    Bantam, 61
    East Grandy, 68
    Hartford, 29
    West Haven, 48

D

Delaware 210
    Cranston Heights, 119
    Dover, 206
    Farmington, 80, 167
    Magnolia, 284

F

Florida
    Fort Meyers, 263
    Homestead, 41
    Moon Lake, 223

G

Georgia
    Camp Gordon, 55

H

Hawaii
    Honolulu, 266
    Maui, 172

I

Idaho
    Boise, 225, 226, 291
    Eagle, 230
    Emmett, 165
    Idaho Falls, 314
    Kuna, 179, 261
    Lewiston, 241
    Madison County, 312
    Middleton, 137
    Mountain House, 235
    Pocatello, 19
    Shoshone County, 212
    Wallace, 49
    Worley, 63
Illinois 234
    Byron, 319
    Chicago, 67, 136, 190, 208, 211
    Dundee, 317
    Dupo, 219
    Forest City, 219
    Freeburg, 284, 308
    Granite City, 149
    Harvard, 315
    Hinsdale, 65
    Lenzburg, 77
    Metropolis, 46, 284
    Rock Island, 186
    Sparta, 308
    Troy Township, 186
Indiana
    Hartford City, 142
    Indianapolis, 93
    Kokomo, 182
    Ligonier, 140

Logansport, 53, 68, 155
Wabash, 53

Iowa
Clarksville, 107
Granger, 216
Jessup, 148
Oakland, 51
Stanton, 62
Tama County, 194
Urbandale, 72
Waterloo, 38

K

Kansas 172
Coffeyville, 50
Kentucky
Dixon, 306
Jeffersonville, 173

L

Louisiana
Many, 195
Thibodaux, 271

M

Maine 60
Bar Harbor, 110
Limestone, 131
Milford, 44
Maryland 317
Baltimore County, 214
Bayden, 261
Bedford Road, 186
Caroline County, 329
Chesapeake City, 173
Chestertown, 281
Cordova, 192, 298, 308
Eastport, 191
Hagerstown, 98
Huntingtown, 319
Hyattstown, 251
Odessa, 292
Pikesville, 298
Port Penn, 303
Queen Anne-Hillsboro, 221
Queenstown, 282
Reisterton, 150
Ridgley, 259
Trappe, 273
Wheaton, 293
Massachusetts
Lenox, 153
Marshfield, 126
Middelboro, 222
Newbury, 16
Springfield, 29, 47
Swansea, 86
Westfield, 29
Michigan
Battle Creek, 95, 220, 221, 247
Charlotte, 321

Coldwater, 141
Detroit, 68, 119, 205
Grand Haven, 112
Grand Ledge, 150
Huntington Woods, 108
Ishpeming, 138
Lakewood, 74
Larchmont Grosse Point Park, 98
Mount Clemens, 266
Mount Pleasant, 108
Parchment, 99
Wyoming, 228
Minnesota 217
Brownton, 96
Crosby, 56
Detroit Lakes, 38
Lake City, 131
Luverne, 213
Minneapolis, 44, 101
Osakis, 101
St. Paul, 75
Mississippi
Tupelo, 39
Missouri
Madison, 73
Manchester, 171
St. Louis, 37, 73, 77, 140, 171, 219, 224
Montana 270
Billings, 253

N

Nebraska 304
Beatrice, 79
Blair, 227
Grand Island, 158, 166
Hooper, 198
Nevada 233
Carson City, 259
Nye County, 85
Panaca, 218
Wells, 175
New 181
New Hampshire
Concord, 69
White Mountain National Forest, 128
Wolfsboro, 225
New Jersey 103
Andover, 127
Belford, 220
Bloomsberg, 155
Brookview, 120
Brunswick, 159
Camdem, 159
Chatham, 133
Cranbury, 123
Deepwater, 174
East Dover, 283
Erlton, 64
Fair Lawn, 70, 139
Folsum, 170
Franklin Township, 304
Gloucester City, 132
Irvington, 70

Island Heights, 231
Lambs Terrace, 171
Landsville, 257
Leesburg, 81
Leonardo, 141
Long Branch, 49, 92
Marlboro, 243
Marmora, 192
Matawan Township, 146
Moonachie, 214, 231
Morestown, 88
Neptune Township, 90
New Brunswick, 202
Oakland, 26
Oaklyn, 223
Ocean Grove, 27, 91, 193
Old Bridge, 88
Piscataway, 121
Pitman, 224
Pocantico Hills, 77
Port Monmouth, 105
Rancocas, 293
Rockaway, 106
Rockleigh, 168
Saddle River, 144
South Vineland, 100
Spring Lake Heights, 211
Stone Harbor, 121
Teaneck, 124
Totowa, 136
Towaco, 102
Wanaque Valley, 50
Waramosa, 93
White House, 104
Wildwood, 215
New Mexico 62
Eagle Nest, 310
New York 200, 210
Binghamton, 89
Buffalo, 27, 89, 122, 154
Clayton, 102
Clifton Park, 165
Cromwell Valley, 275
East Greenbush, 106
Edgewater, 77
Elmira Heights, 125, 180, 199
Elmira, 36
Glenwood Landing, 209
Lancaster, 261
Lindenhurst, 94
Long Island, 118, 157, 220, 242
Lynbrook, 92
Maine, 63
Marlboro, 124
McLean, 279
Nashville, 234
Olean, 299
Oswego, 125
Perry, 110, 127
Port Byron, 103
Queens, 28
Rockaway Point, 273
Rockville Center, 203, 209, 224, 238
Sand Lake, 262
Seneca Falls, 16, 17

Spark Hill, 89
Spring Valley, 238
Staten Island, 26
Syracuse, 102, 103, 284
Tarrytown, 50
Tully, 328
Utica, 80, 88
North Carolina
Fort Barnwell, 263
Henderson, 69, 214
Washington, 276

O

Ohio
Arlington Heights, 156
Cincinnati, 104, 196
Columbus, 132
Conneaut, 328
Dublin, 152
Kilgore, 166
LaFayette, 169
Lima, 44, 45
Parma Heights, 135
Parma, 146
Prospect, 78
Wooster, 251, 328
Youngstown, 54
Oklahoma
Fort Reno, 157
Lawton, 55
Ontario
Brantford, 30
Kingsville, 84
Walkerville, 84
Woodstock, 84
Oregon
Albany, 21
Cornelius, 264, 297, 320
Forest Glen, 265
Junction City, 296
Maupin, 324
Portland, 267, 292
Stayton, 21

P

Pennsylvania
Albion, 64
Allentown, 91
Altoona, 229, 297
Arnold, 142
Beaver County, 252
Blawnox, 154
Bridgeport, 48
Cedar Top, 198
Chester County, 211
Christiana, 75
Curwensville, 197
Dickson City, 109
Erwinna, 228
Flowerton, 105
Folsum, 327
Fort Washington, 105

Grantley, 89
Hatfield, 122
Highland, 117
Kennett Square, 297
Lewistown, 44
Loyalsock, 203
Mars, 185
Nanticoke, 264
Newville, 134
North Warren, 188
North York, 227
Oxford, 305
Parkland, 229
Pittsburgh, 248
Reinerton, 132
Sellersville, 17, 137
Shinglehouse, 309
Stevens, 209
Trumbaversville, 184
Windsor, 151

R

Rhode Island
Providence, 47, 293

S

Saskatchewan
Saskatoon, 26
South Carolina
Sumter National Forest, 116
South Dakota
Rapid City, 46, 289

T

Tennessee
Adamsville, 224
Bartlett, 171
Chickasaw Village, 167, 184
Clarksville, 256
Fisherville, 168
Jackson, 76
Knox County, 326
Lexington, 232
Milan, 180
Obion, 143
Texas
Burnett, 117
Camp Travis, 55
Conroe, 290
Hondo, 101
San Antonio, 101
Wichita Falls, 37

U

Utah
Heber City, 275
Heber Valley, 280
Sandy City, 286

V

Vermont
Barwick, 69
Johnson, 285
Montpelier, 285
Washington, 293
Virginia
Ashland, 296
Roanoke, 173, 184
Warrenton, 196

W

Washington 297
Asotin, 325
Auburn, 286
College Place, 235
Everson, 303
Rockford, 241
Seattle, 118, 218
Snohomish, 145
Spokane, 145
West Valley, 320
West Virginia 152
Salem, 90
Vienna, 179
Wisconsin
Amherst, 120
Appleton, 54, 290, 311
Bear Creek, 85
Black River Falls, 20, 97, 149
Bowler, 112
Boyd, 107
Brown Deer, 318
Clintonville, 138
Ephraim, 327
Gilman, 95
Hartford, 47
Hurley, 178
Iola, 54, 153
Kenosha, 56, 70
Marion, 189, 311
Menomonie, 213
New Glarus, 15
Oconto Falls, 139
Richfield, 108
Ridgeland, 282
Sauk City, 85
Shawano, 327
Sparta, 96, 140
Stoughton, 47, 107
West Allis, 51
West Bend, 138
Wyoming 258
Goshen County, 267

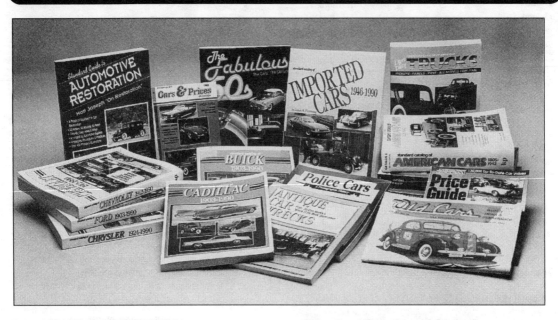